FOCUSED READING

Kyung Suk Kim

Shinasa

* This book was supported by Kyonggi University Research Grant in 2012.

Foreword

Reading requires so much more than just understanding the meaning of words and grammar. It is particularly so for reading for academic purposes. Through active engagement with the different uses of words and varied realizations of grammar in reading texts, linguistic and cultural background knowledge can be accumulated and applied to other reading tasks. With no such background knowledge, it is difficult to understand academic reading materials. The best route to acquire linguistic and cultural background knowledge is to read extensively a wide variety of genres.

Focused Reading is designed to help you have an access to a broad range of topics accompanied by after-reading activities structured and detailed enough for self-study to boost your linguistic and cultural background knowledge. For those who feel insecure in studying by themselves, sample answer keys are available for most close-ended activities. Ten topic areas are chosen and under each topic, several reading texts are presented with a wide range of activities which include filling in the blanks, T/F questions, focused grammar, collocational use, changing parts of speech, using key words in different contexts, cross-word puzzle, analyzing coreferential relationship, and so many more.

Reading is in reality taught with a mostly teacher-centered method. However, the discovery of meaning and the accumulation of background knowledge through self-guided understanding of reading texts have far-reaching effects on language learning.

I hope you find ***Focused Reading*** enjoyable.

Kyung Suk Kim

Contents

Chapter 1

Food and Health

Green guava

A green guava is sour and hard. You bite into it at its widest point, because it's easier to grasp with your teeth. You hear the skin, meat, and seeds crunching inside your head, while the inside of your mouth explodes in little **spurts*** of sour. You **grimace***, your eyes water, and your cheeks disappear as your lips **purse*** into an O. But you have another and then another, enjoying the crunchy sounds, the acid taste, the **gritty*** **texture*** of the unripe center. At night, your mother makes you drink **castor oil***, which she says tastes better than a green guava. That's when you know for sure that you're a child and she has stopped being one.

I had my last guava the day we left Puerto Rico. It was large and juicy, almost red in the center, and so fragrant that I didn't want to eat it because I would lose the smell. All the way to the airport I scratched at it with my teeth, making little dents in the skin, chewing small pieces with my front teeth, so that I could feel the texture against my tongue, the tiny pink **pellets*** of sweet.

Today, I stand before a stack of dark green guavas, each perfectly round and hard, each $1.59. The one in my hand is tempting. It smells faintly of late summer afternoons and **hopscotch*** under the mango tree. But this is autumn in New York, and I'm no longer a child.

1 Key Vocabulary

spurt ***n.*** a sudden short burst
grimace ***v.*** to make a facial expression usually of disgust, disapproval, or pain
purse ***v.*** to tighten one's lips into a rounded shape
gritty ***adj.*** containing or covered with very small pieces of stone or sand
texture ***n.*** the way something feels when touched or eaten
castor oil ***n.*** a thick colorless or yellow oil that is obtained from the seeds of the castor oil plant. It has a very unpleasant taste and in former times was used as a medicine and industrially as a lubricant.

pellet ***n.*** a small rounded body

hopscotch ***n.*** a children's game in which players toss a small object into the numbered spaces of a pattern of rectangles outlined on the ground and then hop or jump through the spaces to retrieve the object

2 Complete the sentence with the correct form of the words in the box.

dent(*n.*), grasp(*v.*), unripe, scratch(*v.*), tempting, crunch(*v.*)

a. Depending on your choice, ___________ fruit can either be a delicious, nutritious treat or a problem to your stomach.
b. Six residents of Wilmington have been bitten or ___________ by a cat.
c. What is forbidden is always ___________.
d. There are many different actors that ___________ my attention for one reason or another.
e. Someone made a huge ___________ in my car and drove away.
f. Jimmy walked to the table, picked up a carrot, ___________ it loudly as he leaned leisurely against the table.

Neapolitan pizza

The innovation that gave us the flat bread we call pizza was the use of tomato as a topping. For some time after the tomato was brought to Europe from the Americas in the 16th century, it was believed by many Europeans to be poisonous(as are some other fruits of the **nightshade*** family). However, by the late 18th century, it was common for the poor of the area around Naples to add tomato to their yeast-based flat bread, and so the pizza was born. The dish gained in popularity, and soon pizza became a tourist attraction as visitors to Naples ventured into the poorer areas of the city to try the local specialty. Until about 1830, pizza was sold from open-air stands and out of pizza bakeries. Pizzerias keep this old tradition alive today. It is possible to enjoy pizza wrapped in paper and a drink sold from open-air stands outside the **premises***. Antica Pizzeria Port'Alba in Naples is widely regarded as the city's first pizzeria. It started producing pizzas for **peddlers*** in 1738 but expanded to a pizza restaurant with chairs and tables in 1830. It still serves pizza from the same premises today.

A description of pizza in Naples around 1830 is given by the French writer and food expert Alexandre Dumas, in his work *Le Corricolo*, Chapter VIII. He writes pizza was the only food of the humble people in Naples during winter and that "in Naples pizza is flavored with cheese, tomato, tallow, oil, lard, or anchovies."

The Neapolitans take their pizza very seriously. Purists, like the famous pizzeria Da Michele(founded 1870), consider there to be only two true pizzas—the Marinara and the Margherita—and that is all they serve. These two "pure" pizzas are the ones preferred by many Italians today. The

Marinara is the older of the two and has a topping of tomato, oregano, garlic and extra virgin olive oil. It is named "Marinara" not because it has seafood on it(it doesn't) but because it was the food prepared by "la marinara," the seaman's wife, for her **seafaring*** husband when he returned from fishing trips in the Bay of Naples. The Margherita, topped with modest amounts of tomato sauce, mozzarella cheese and fresh basil is widely attributed to baker Raffaele Esposito. Esposito worked at the pizzeria "Pietro... e basta così" (literally "Peter... and that's enough"), which was established in 1880, and is still operating under the name "Pizzeria Brandi." In 1889, he baked three different pizzas for the visit of King Umberto I and Queen Margherita of Savoy. The Queen's favorite was a pizza **evoking*** the colors of the Italian flag—green(basil leaves), white(mozzarella), and red(tomatoes). This combination was named Pizza Margherita in her honor.

"Associazione Verace Pizza Napoletana"(True Neapolitan Pizza Association), which was founded in 1984 and only recognizes the Marinara and Margherita verace, has set the very specific rules that must be followed for an authentic Neapolitan pizza. These include that the pizza must be baked in a wood-fired, domed oven at 485℃ for no more than 60 to 90 seconds; that the base must be **hand-kneaded*** and must not be rolled with a pin or prepared by any mechanical means and that the pizza must not exceed 35 centimeters in diameter or be more than one-third of a centimeter thick at the center. The association also selects pizzerias all around the world to produce and spread the verace pizza napoletana philosophy and method.

There are many famous pizzerias in Naples where these traditional pizzas can be found like Da Michele, Port'Alba, Brandi, Di Matteo, Sorbillo, Trianon and Umberto. Most of them are in the ancient historical center of Naples. These pizzerias will go even further than the specified rules by, for example, only using "San Marzano" tomatoes grown on the slopes of Mount Vesuvius and only **drizzling*** the olive oil and adding tomato topping in a clockwise direction.

1 Key Vocabulary

nightshade *n.* any of numerous plants of the genus *Solanum*, most of which have poisonous juice though many bear edible fruit
premises *n.* land and the buildings on it; a building or part of a building
peddler *n.* someone who sells something outside or by going from place to place to find customers
seafaring *adj.* working or traveling regularly on the ocean
evoke *v.* to call to mind
hand-knead *v.* to make or shape by folding, pressing, and stretching with the hands
drizzle *v.* to pour a small amount of liquid over food that you are preparing

2 Add a suffix to each word and complete the sentences with the new words.

-ally	-able	-ive	-ity	-ize	-ly	-al

tradition_____ attract_____ popular_____(*n.*) literal_____
prefer_____ special_____(*v.*) attribute_____ specific_____(*adv.*)

a. There is nothing more __________ than good skin without thick make-up.
b. Numerous deaths from lung disease are __________ to smoking.
c. I think that the program's __________ is down to two things.
d. Their wedding ceremony is a delicate balance between __________ and contemporary values.
e. She __________ in women's health issues, including mood and anxiety.
f. There are some companies that publish hotel guides, __________ for business travelers.
g. Some people find that seeing one doctor all the way through is __________ to having a different doctor each time, as it provides consistency.
h. There were __________ thousands of people waiting outside the football stadium.

3 Famous Quotes about Pizza

Q My fellow Americans, ask not what your pizza can do for you; ask what you can do for your pizza. — Anonymous

Q There's no better feeling in the world than a warm pizza box on your lap. — Kevin James

Q God ordered the world and all things in it, and I ordered a pizza and all things on it. — Jarod Kintz

Q Any time you have large numbers of people together? And the TV on? Pizza works because it's so easy to share. — Jeremy White

Q We live in an age when pizza gets to your home before the police. — Jeff Marder

Q The only thing we have to fear is a lack of pizza. — Anonymous

Cross-word puzzle

Across

1. to distribute widely
6. a product of a distinctive kind
7. somewhere that is interesting
9. to flatten
10. low in rank
12. a building or part of a building

Down

1. an upward or downward direction
2. having a claimed origin
3. to dare to go
4. capable of killing
5. distance from side to side of a circle
8. an addition on top of a dish
11. to bring into the mind

An unusual shopper

A youngish man, a **trifle*** overweight, too anxious for his age, completed his circuit of the supermarket shelves and cabinets and stood in line, ashamed as usual. He arranged his purchases on the checkout belt and waited, with his eye fixed on the street beyond the shop window, while the woman at the **till*** scanned all the bar codes on his medicines, his vitamins, his air freshener, his toilet tissue, his frozen Meals for One, his tins, his magazines, his beer, and his deodorant, his bread, bananas, milk, his fat-free yogurt, his jar of decaf, and his treats: today, some roasted chicken legs, some grapes, a block of chocolate, and two croissants. He rubbed his thumb along the **embossed*** numbers of his credit card while each item triggered a **trill*** of recognition from the till.

The till's computer recognized the young man's Distinctive Shopping Fingerprint as well, the usual ratio of fat to **starch***, the familiar selection of canned food, the recent and increasing range of health supplements, and the unique combination of monthly magazines. The pattern of shopping identified the customer. Even before the woman at the till had **swiped*** the credit card, the computer had lined up the young man's details—his list of purchases for the previous seven months, his credit rating, his Customer Loyalty score.

It knew broadly who he was and how he lived. It could deduce what his modest rooms above the travel shop were like, how stale they were, how flowerless, how functional, how crying out for change. Here was the man whose cat had died or run away three months ago. No cat food purchased since that time. Here was the customer who had not left the neighborhood for more than seven days in living, byte-sized memory. Last spring, he'd tried and failed to cut down on **patisseries*** and sugar. Today, for once, he had resisted his usual impulse purchase of a packet of **cheroots***.

Computer screened a message on the woman's till: Cheroots ... Cheroots

... it said. Remind the customer he has not purchased cereals or cheese or vegetables this month. Remind him of our *special offers*: 12 cans of lager for the price of 10. Buy one bottle of our Boulevard liqueur and get a second free. Remind him that time is passing more quickly than he thinks—his washing powder should be used by now, as should the contraceptives that he bought two years ago. He must need basics, such as rice and pasta, soap, toothpaste, flour, oil and **condiments***. Inform him of our Retail Schemes and that we open now on Sunday afternoons. Advise him that he ought to do more cooking for himself. He ought to tidy up and clean the bathroom tiles with our new lemon whitener. He ought to start afresh. Suggest to him he tour our shelves again. At once. For what we choose is what we are. He should not miss this second opportunity to re-create himself with food.

1 Key Vocabulary

trifle ***adv.*** slightly
till ***n.*** a cash register; a money drawer in a store or bank
embossed ***adj.*** decorated with raised design
trill ***n.*** a sound similar to a musical trill(singing or playing two similar notes one after the other very quickly), made by a bird or a piece of electronic equipment
starch ***n.*** a white substance without any taste that is chiefly found in rice, potatoes, and other vegetables; a type of carbohydrate that gives you energy
swipe ***v.*** to pass a plastic card through an electronic reader
patisseries ***n.*** pastries sold at a bakery specializing French pastry

cheroot ***n.*** a cigar with both ends cut flat
condiment ***n.*** something used to improve the flavor of food

2 Match the expression in column A with the related product/ situation in column B.

A	B
1. his tins	protein shake, calcium
2. health supplements	beer, malt liquor
3. his modest rooms ... how crying out for change	toothbrush, shampoo
4. 12 cans of lager	untidy, messed up
5. He must need basics ...	canned soups or tuna

3 Imagine you are the man and your partner is the woman at the till. Have a conversation about the items you bought.

Things to remember when cooking fish

The three most important things to remember when cooking fish are "don't overcook", "don't over-season", and "keep it moist"! As a rule of thumb, fish should be cooked 12 minutes per inch in thickness, but this will vary depending on cooking method. A fish is done when the **translucency*** in the center of the fillet is almost gone. Use a **paring knife*** to test. Also, don't forget that fresh fish should be cooked simply so its flavor stands alone. A touch of butter and lemon may be all you need. Lastly, different types of fish require different cooking techniques. Use the technique that will keep your fillet moist and tender. In general, a leaner fish needs moist heat while a fattier one does not.

Tips for Grilling Fish

Fish steaks and fillets should be at least 1/2 inch in thickness when grilling, and may or may not need a **marinade***, depending on the species or the chef. A firm-fleshed fish is always a good choice for the grill because it holds together well. Always quickly **sear*** both sides of a fish steak or fillet over the hottest portion of the grill and then move to the edges to finish the cooking. Again, the hotter and faster the better!

Tips on Baking Fish

Simply stated, fish should be baked in a 425°F oven for 12 minutes per inch of thickness. Fattier fish, like salmon or black cod, need very little additional fat like oil or butter, while leaner fish do.

Tips For Pan-Searing Fish

Pan-frying or pan-searing are two of the easiest methods for cooking fish. Simply add oil or butter to a non-stick pan, lightly season and cook over medium heat. In general, the thinner the fillet, the higher the heat. If a thick fillet is cooked at too high of a heat, the outside will burn and the inside will remain raw.

1 Key Vocabulary

translucency ***n.*** the quality of admitting rays of light to pass through, but not so as to make objects distinguishable

paring knife ***n.*** A paring knife is a small knife with a plain edge blade that is ideal for peeling and other small or intricate work (such as removing seeds, slicing garlic or cutting mango). It is designed to be an all-purpose knife, similar to a chef's knife, except smaller. Paring knives are usually between 6 and 10cm(2½ and 4 inches) long.

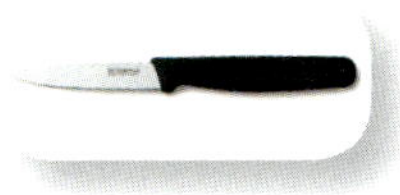

marinade ***n.*** a liquid mixture, usually of vinegar or wine and oil with various spices and herbs, in which meat, fish, or vegetables are soaked before cooking

sear ***v.*** to burn slightly and superficially

2 Which of the following is NOT true according to the passage?

a. Both a leaner fish and a fattier one need moist heat.
b. A firm-fleshed fish is a good choice for the grill because it can be cooked in a short period of time.
c. If a fish is 2 inches thick, it should be baked in a 425°F oven for 20 minutes.
d. When pan-frying fish, the thinner the fillet is, the higher the heat should be.

3 Abbreviations and acronyms commonly used in cooking

BBQ = barbecued	IC = immediate consumption
BP = baking powder	lg = large
btr = butter	mayo = mayonnaise
cal = calories	nonf = nonfat
cnd = canned	RED PEP = red pepper
F&B = food and beverage	sm = small
FF = fast food	T or tbsp = tablespoon
flvr = flavor	t or tsp = teaspoon
frz = frozen	wtr = water
gm = gram	x = extra

Cross-word puzzle(names of popular foods)

Across

3. I had a chocolate m______ as breakfast.
4. Does eating ______ help weight loss?
6. My favorite ______ is from McDonald.
9. the most famous Japanese dish
10. I love ______ chips so much.
11. A ______ is a traditional Mexican dish composed of a corn or wheat tortilla folded or rolled around a filling.

Down

1. She ate the last slice of ______.
2. Farmers grow ______ in the rich soil.
4. ______ is a solid food made from milk.
5. A chicken lays an ______ per day.
7. a yellow tropical fruit
8. This low fat ______ has only 1% fat.

Sick building syndrome

What Is Sick Building Syndrome?

Sick building syndrome (SBS) is a situation in which occupants of a building experience **acute*** health effects that seem to be linked to time spent in a building, but no specific illness or cause can be identified. The complaints may be localized in a particular room or zone, or may be widespread throughout the building. Frequently, problems result when a building is operated or maintained in a manner that is inconsistent with its original design or **prescribed*** operating procedures. Sometimes indoor air problems are a result of poor building design or occupant activities.

What Are the Symptoms of SBS?

Building occupants complain of symptoms associated with acute discomfort. These symptoms include headaches; eye, nose, and throat irritation; a dry cough; dry or itchy skin; dizziness and nausea; difficulty in concentrating; fatigue; and sensitivity to odors. With SBS, no clinically defined disease or specific chemical or biological **contaminant*** can be determined as the cause of the symptoms. Most of the complainants feel relief soon after leaving the building. SBS reduces worker productivity and may also increase **absenteeism***.

What Causes SBS?

While specific causes of SBS remain unknown, the following have been cited as contributing factors to sick building syndrome. These elements may act in combination or may supplement other complaints such as inadequate temperature, humidity, or lighting.

• Chemical contaminants from outdoor sources: Outdoor air that enters a building can also be a source of indoor pollution. Pollutants from motor vehicle **exhausts***, plumbing **vents***, and building exhausts (bathrooms and kitchens) can enter the building through poorly located air intake vents, windows, and other openings. **Combustion*** byproducts can also enter a building from a nearby garage.

• Chemical contaminants from indoor sources: Most indoor air pollution comes from sources inside the building. For example, adhesives, upholstery, carpeting, copy machines, manufactured wood products, cleaning agents and pesticides may emit **volatile*** organic compounds (VOCs) including formaldehyde. Research shows that some VOCs can cause chronic and acute health effects at high concentrations, and some are known **carcinogens***. Low to moderate levels of multiple VOCs may also produce acute reactions in some individuals. Environmental tobacco smoke and combustion products from stoves, fireplaces, and unvented space heaters all can put chemical contaminants into the air.

• Biological contaminants: Biological contaminants include pollen, bacteria, viruses, and molds. These contaminants can breed in **stagnant*** water that has accumulated in humidifiers and ducts, or where water has collected on ceiling tiles, insulation, or carpet. Biological contaminants can cause fever, chills, cough, chest tightness, muscle aches, and allergic reactions. One indoor air bacterium, Legionella, has caused both Pontiac Fever and Legionnaire's Disease.

• Inadequate ventilation: In the 1970s the oil **embargo*** led building designers to make buildings more airtight, with less outdoor air ventilation, in order to improve energy efficiency. These reduced ventilation rates have been found to be, in many cases, inadequate to maintain the health and comfort of building occupants.

What Are the Solutions to Sick Building Syndrome?

Solutions to SBS problems usually include combinations of the following measures:

• Increasing the ventilation rates and air distribution is often a cost-effective means of reducing indoor pollutant levels. At a minimum, heating, ventilating, and air conditioning systems should be designed to meet ventilation standards in local building codes. Make sure that the system is operated and maintained to ensure that the design ventilation rates are attained. If there are strong pollutant sources, air may need to be vented directly to the outside. This method is especially recommended to remove pollutants that accumulate in specific areas such as restrooms, copy rooms, and printing facilities.

• Removal or modification of the pollutant source is the most effective approach to solving a known source of an indoor air quality problem when this solution is practicable. Ways to do this include replacing water-stained ceiling tiles and carpets; banning smoking or providing a separately ventilated room; venting contaminant source emissions to the outdoors; using and storing paints, solvents, pesticides, and adhesives in closed containers in well-ventilated areas; using those pollutant sources in periods of low or no occupancy; and allowing time for building materials in new or remodeled areas to **off-gas*** pollutants before occupancy.

• Air cleaning has some limitations, but it can be a useful addition to source control and ventilation. Air filters are only effective at removing some, not all, of the pollution.

• Education and communication are important parts of any air quality management program. When everyone associated with the building, from occupants to maintenance, fully understands the issues and communicates with each other, they can work more effectively together to prevent and solve problems.

1 Key Vocabulary

acute ***adj.*** arising suddenly and becoming severe
prescribe ***v.*** to state officially what should be done in a particular situation
contaminant ***n.*** a material that makes something less pure
absenteeism ***n.*** the habit of not being at work when you should be
exhaust ***n.*** gases from the engine of a car as it works
vent ***n.*** an opening for the escape of a gas or liquid
combustion ***n.*** the act of burning
volatile ***adj.*** flying or having the power to fly
carcinogen ***n.*** a substance that causes cancer
stagnant ***adj.*** not moving; not growing or developing

embargo ***n.*** a government order to stop something, especially trading
off-gas ***v.*** to slowly release chemicals

2 Write the adverb form of each of the following adjectives. Then complete the sentences with the correct adverb.

specific ________	inadequate ________	chronic ________
separate ________	increasing ________	effective ________

a. In an age when competition is ________ stiff, personal contact will become the critical factor in determining corporate success.
b. The Army has just finished testing combat uniforms designed ________ for women, only.
c. What do you think is the best way to ________ communicate in the workplace?
d. The current social care system is ________ funded. People are not receiving the care and support that they deserve.
e. Sometimes people get into bad habits because they are either ________ tired all the time, or simply don't feel that well in general.
f. Applicants may enter as many times as they wish, but each entry must be sent ________.

3 Have you ever heard of these syndromes?

Münchausen Syndrome

The affected person exaggerates or creates symptoms of illnesses in themselves to gain investigation, treatment, attention, and comfort from medical personnel. In some extreme cases, people suffering from Münchausen syndrome are highly knowledgeable about the practice of medicine and are able to produce symptoms that result in lengthy and costly medical analysis, prolonged hospital stay and unnecessary operations.

New World Syndrome

It is a set of non-transmittable diseases brought on by consumption of junk food. Native Americans, the indigenous people of Oceania and perhaps other people of Asian origin are susceptible. It is characterized by obesity, heart disease, diabetes and shortened life span, and, of course, by a change from a traditional diet and exercise to a modern diet.

Paris Syndrome

It is a temporary psychological disorder encountered by certain people, in most cases from Japan visiting Paris. It is characterized by a number of psychiatric symptoms such as feelings of persecution (perceptions of being a victim of prejudice, aggression, or hostility from others), depersonalization, anxiety, dizziness, sweating, and others.

Stockholm Syndrome

It is a psychological phenomenon in which hostages express empathy and have positive feelings towards their captors, sometimes to the point of defending them. The FBI's Hostage Barricade Database System shows that roughly 27% of victims show evidence of Stockholm Syndrome.

Eating disorders

Eating disorders are more than just going on a diet to lose weight or trying to exercise every day. They're extremes in eating behavior—the diet that never ends and gradually gets more restrictive, for example. Or the person who can't go out with friends because he or she thinks it's more important to go running to work off a snack eaten earlier. The most common eating disorders are anorexia **nervosa*** and bulimia nervosa (usually called simply "anorexia" and "bulimia"). But other food-related disorders, like binge eating, body image disorders, and food phobias, are becoming more and more common.

People with anorexia have a real fear of weight gain and a distorted view of their body size and shape. As a result, they can't maintain a normal body weight. Many teens with anorexia restrict their food intake by dieting, fasting, or excessive exercise. They hardly eat at all—and the small amount of food they do eat becomes an obsession. Others with anorexia may start binge eating and purging—eating a lot of food and then trying to get rid of the calories by forcing themselves to vomit, using **laxatives***, or exercising excessively, or some combination of these.

Bulimia is similar to anorexia. With bulimia, someone might binge eat and then try to compensate in extreme ways, such as forced vomiting or excessive exercise, to prevent weight gain. Over time, these steps can be dangerous—both physically and emotionally. They can also lead to compulsive behaviors (ones that are hard to stop). To be diagnosed with bulimia, a person must be binging and purging regularly, at least twice a week for a couple of months. Binge eating is different from going to a party and **pigging out*** on pizza, then deciding to go to the gym the next day and eat more healthfully. People with bulimia eat a large amount of food at once, usually in secret. Sometimes they eat food that is not cooked or

might be still frozen, or retrieve food from the trash. They typically feel powerless to stop the eating and can only stop once they're too full to eat any more. Most people with bulimia then purge by vomiting, but may also use laxatives or excessive exercise.

Although anorexia and bulimia are very similar, people with anorexia are usually very thin and underweight but those with bulimia may be a normal weight or can be overweight. Fortunately, eating disorders can be treated. People with eating disorders can get well and gradually learn to eat well and more like their family and friends again. Eating disorders involve both the mind and body. So medical doctors, mental health professionals, and dietitians will often be involved in a person's treatment and recovery. Therapy or counseling is a very important part of getting better—in many cases, family therapy is one of the keys to eating healthily again. Parents and other family members are important in supporting people who have to regain weight that they are afraid of, or to learn to accept the body shape that their culture, genes, and lifestyle allow for.

If you want to talk to someone about eating disorders but are unable or not ready to talk to a parent or close family member, try reaching out to a friend, teacher, school nurse or counselor, your doctor, or another trusted adult. Remember that eating disorders are very common among teens. Treatment options depend on each person and their families, but many treatments incorporate **journaling***, talking to therapists, and working with dietitians and other professionals. Learning to be comfortable at your healthy weight is a process. It takes time to **unlearn*** some behaviors and relearn others. Be patient, you can learn to like your body, understand your eating behaviors, and figure out the relationship between feelings and eating—all the tools you need to feel in control and to like and accept yourself for who you are.

1 Key Vocabulary

nervosa ***n.*** something that affects the nervous system, mental capacity, or reasoning

laxative ***n.*** a medicine which makes it easier to pass waste matter from the bowels

pig out ***v.*** to overeat; to eat immodestly

journal *v.* to record something
unlearn *v.* to try to forget; to put out of one's memory or knowledge

2 Famous Quotes about Health

- **Q** Some people think that doctors and nurses can put scrambled eggs back into the shell. — Dorothy Canfield Fisher
- **Q** I have never yet met a healthy person who worried very much about his health, or a really good person who worried much about his own soul. — John B. S. Haldane
- **Q** A man's health can be judged by which he takes two at a time—pills or stairs. — Joan Welsh
- **Q** Be careful about reading health books. You may die of a misprint. — Mark Twain
- **Q** A man too busy to take care of his health is like a mechanic too busy to take care of his tools. — Spanish Proverb
- **Q** The biggest seller is cookbooks and the second is diet books—how not to eat what you've just learned how to cook. — Andy Rooney
- **Q** The way to keep your health is to eat what you don't want, drink what you don't like, and do what you'd rather not. — Mark Twain
- **Q** You have to stay in shape. My grandmother, she started walking five miles a day when she was 60. She's 97 today and we don't know where the hell she is. — Ellen DeGeneres

Now write your own statement about health.

3 Fill in the blanks with the appropriate word from the words below. Use each word only once.

desperately	self-induced	compensate
slightly	weigh	quantities

Many people with anorexia nervosa see themselves as overweight, even when they are clearly underweight. Eating, food, and weight control become obsessions. People with anorexia nervosa typically (1)__________ themselves repeatedly, portion food carefully, and eat very small (2)__________ of only certain foods. Some people with anorexia nervosa may also engage in binge-eating followed by extreme dieting, excessive exercise, (3)__________ vomiting, and/or misuse of laxatives, or diuretics.

Bulimia nervosa is characterized by recurrent and frequent episodes of eating unusually large amounts of food and feeling a lack of control over these episodes. This binge-eating is followed by actions that (4)__________ for the overeating such as forced vomiting, excessive use of laxatives or diuretics, fasting, excessive exercise, or a combination of these behaviors. Unlike anorexia nervosa, people with bulimia nervosa usually maintain what is considered a healthy or normal weight, while some are (5)__________ overweight. But like people with anorexia nervosa, they often fear gaining weight, want (6)__________ to lose weight, and are intensely unhappy with their body size and shape.

Chapter 2

Job

My first job

I thought I'd find an easy job, the kind other kids had, working in the dime store or maybe a hotdog **stand***. And though I hadn't started working yet, I thought I might the week after the next. But when I came home that afternoon, all wet because Tito had pushed me into the open water **hydrant***—**only*** I had sort of let him—Mama called me in the kitchen before I could even go and change, and Aunt Lala was sitting there drinking her coffee with a spoon. Aunt Lala said she had found a job for me at the Peter Pan Restaurant where she worked, and how old was I, and to show up tomorrow saying I was one year older, and that was that. So the next morning I put on the navy blue dress that made me look older and borrowed money for lunch and bus fare because Aunt Lala said I wouldn't get paid till the next Friday, and I went in and saw the boss of the Peter Pan Restaurant and lied about my age like Aunt Lala told me to and **sure enough***, I started working that same day.

1 Key Vocabulary

stand ***n.*** a booth for the display of goods for sale
hydrant ***n.*** a pipe connected to the main water supply especially in a street
only ***conj*****.** except that; however
sure enough ***idiom.*** as one might have expected; certainly

2 Find synonyms for these words from the text.

a. supervisor	b. obtain	c. shove
d. misinform	e. undemanding	f. booth

3 Complete the blanks in the following descriptions of jobs using the appropriate words.

harbourmasters	conductors	architects
flight attendants	foresters	security guards

a. ______________ provide services in connection with the design and construction of buildings and the space within the site surrounding the buildings.

b. ______________ are responsible for enforcing the regulations of a particular port in order to ensure the safety of navigation, the security of the port and the correct operation of the port facilities.

c. ______________ are members of an aircrew employed by airlines primarily to ensure the safety and comfort of passengers aboard commercial flights, on select business jet aircraft, and on some military aircraft.

d. ______________ protect property by maintaining a high visibility presence to deter illegal and inappropriate actions, observing for signs of crime, fire or disorder; then taking action and reporting any incidents to their client and emergency services as appropriate.

e. ______________ are railway train crew members responsible for operational and safety duties that do not involve actual operation of the train.

f. ____________ practice timber harvesting, ecological restoration and management of protected areas.

Working from home could save billions

Strategic Workstyles 2000, an Oxford forecasting unit, says that industry could make huge financial savings by allowing their staff to work from home. Noel Hodson, the report's author, says that the effects of allowing 15 percent of Britain's 22 million workforce to work in their own homes using telephones, fax machines and computers would be enormous.

London would feel the biggest benefits with 526,000 fewer drivers on the roads. More than 11,000 commuters would not need to enter central London daily. Commuters would benefit from seeing their families more, saving up to four hours a day travelling to work. Companies would have a fresher workforce which did not need to be transported into a central, expensive location daily.

A study for a big financial institution planning to allow 20 people to **telecommute*** calculated that the company would save more than ₤430,000 per year. The study examines the reasons why telecommuting has not achieved the advantages of time saved and cost cutting. It says the managers are often nervous about leaving staff unattended and out of sight of the office. For the 'teleworker', working from home might bring **unforeseen*** hazards, such as a partner who does not want the house invaded by machinery and office paperwork. 'A number of car commuters thoroughly enjoy the total isolation and privacy available to them in their cars,' the report says.

1 Key Vocabulary

telecommute ***v.*** to work at home using a computer connected to the network of one's employer

unforeseen ***adj.*** not felt or realized beforehand; unexpected

2 Famous Quotes about Work

Q By working faithfully eight hours a day, you may eventually get to be a boss and work 12 hours a day. — Robert Frost

Q One machine can do the work of 50 ordinary men. No machine can do the work of one extraordinary man. — Anonymous

Q Miracles sometimes occur, but one has to work terribly hard for them.— Chaim Weizmann

Q The man with the best job in the country is the vice-president. All he has to do is get up every morning and say, "How is the president?" — Will Rogers

Q Rest is the sweet sauce of labour. — Plutarch

Q Every morning I get up and look through the Forbes list of the richest people in America. If I'm not there, I go to work. — Robert Orben

Q Never turn down a job because you think it's too small; you never know where it may lead. — Julia Morgan

Q Too bad all the people who know how to run the country are busy driving taxicabs and cutting hair. — George Burns

Q If a man wakes up famous, he hasn't been sleeping. — Wes Izzard

Q It's amazing how important your job is when you want the day off—and how unimportant it is when you want a raise. — Robert Orben

3 Write down some possible difficulties that the teleworkers might face.

____

____

____

4 Read the following text and choose the most appropriate words for the blanks.

The worst person to work with

At work you'll find plenty of bad _____1_____: the gossip, the chronically tardy person, the kiss-up, and everyone else you try to avoid. Perhaps the one _____2_____ you want to avoid (hanging around and being) more than any other is the negative person. The negative person _____3_____ everything. Every task is too lowly; every meeting lasts too long; every co-worker is too _____4_____. Nary a word passes through his or her _____5_____ that's not dripping with sarcasm. If you realize that you are this furrow-browed employee, the chorus of sighs and complaints, accented with eye rolls, will earn you the worst _____6_____ of everyone. And whether or not you're aware, your boss will _____7_____, too.

1. a. habits	b. feelings	c. traits
2. a. situation	b. type	c. mistake
3. a. pursues	b. hates	c. judges
4. a. dumb	b. competitive	c. happy
5. a. head	b. body	c. lips
6. a. reputation	b. intention	c. behavior
7. a. understand	b. notice	c. appreciate

5 **Imagine that you know a person like the one in the text above. Write a short letter of advice to him/her.**

The young practitioner

May I venture to contrast youth and experience in medical practice? The young man knows the rules, but the old man knows the exceptions. The young man knows his patient, but the old man knows also his patient's family, dead and alive, up and down for generations. He can tell beforehand what diseases their unborn children will be **subject*** to, what they will die of if they live long enough, and whether they had better live at all or remain unrealized possibilities. The young man feels uneasy if he is not continually doing something to stir up his patient's internal arrangements. The old man takes things more quietly, and is much more willing to let well enough alone. All these superiorities, if such they are, you must wait for time to bring you. In the meanwhile, the young man's senses are quicker than those of his older rival. His education in all the accessary **branches*** is more recent, and therefore nearer the existing condition of knowledge. He finds it easier than his seniors to accept the improvements which every year is bringing forward. New ideas build their nests in young men's brains. "Revolutions are not made by men in spectacles," as I once heard it remarked, and the first whispers of a new truth are not caught by those who begin to feel the need of an **ear trumpet***. Granting all these advantages to the young man, he ought, nevertheless, to go on improving, on the whole, as a medical practitioner, with every year, until he has ripened into a well-mellowed maturity. But, to improve, he must be good for something at the start. If you ship a poor **cask*** of wine to India and if you keep it half a century, it only grows thinner and sharper.

1 Key Vocabulary

subject ***adj.*** likely to be affected by something
branch ***n.*** a part of a particular area of knowledge or study

ear trumpet ***n.*** a horn-shaped device formerly used to direct sound into the ear of a hearing-impaired person.

cask ***n.*** a round wooden container for storing a liquid

2 Does each of the following sentences refer to an old practitioner or a young one?

a. He finds it easier than his rival to accept the improvements which every year is bringing forward. __________
b. He can tell beforehand what diseases an unborn children will be subject to. __________
c. His senses are quicker than those of his rival. __________
d. He knows the exceptions in medical practice. __________
e. He feels uneasy if he is not continually doing something to stir up his patient's internal arrangements. __________

3 Who do you prefer? Would you like to visit an old doctor or a young one when you think your memory is falling? Write a reason for your choice.

4 Match the medical occupations with the related conditions/diseases.

Medical Occupations	Conditions/Diseases They Treat
1. cardiologist	a. foot injury
2. dermatologist	b. pregnancy
3. neurologist	c. tumor
4. obstetrician	d. cough
5. orthopedist	e. memory loss
6. oncologist	f. heart attack
7. physician	g. pimple
8. podiatrist	h. broken bone

HUMOR

Joe has been seeing a psychoanalyst for four years for treatment of the fear that he had monsters under his bed. It had been years since he had gotten a good night's sleep. Furthermore, his progress was very poor, and he knew it. So, one day he stops seeing the psychoanalyst and decides to try something different.

A few weeks later, Joe's former psychoanalyst meets his old client in the supermarket, and is surprised to find him looking well-rested, energetic, and cheerful. "Doc!" Joe says, "It's amazing! I'm cured!"

"That's great news!" the psychoanalyst says. "You seem to be doing much better. How?"

"I went to see another doctor," Joe says enthusiastically, "and he cured me in just ONE session!"

"One?!" the psychoanalyst asks incredulously.

"Yeah," continues Joe, "my new doctor is a behaviorist."

"A behaviorist?" the psychoanalyst asks. "How did he cure you in one session?"

"Oh, easy," says Joe. "He told me to cut the legs off of my bed."

Chapter 3

Psychology

Is your partner lying to you?

Trust is the foundation of any lasting relationship, and that's difficult when you suspect your partner is lying. If you already feel suspicious, here are five simple steps to spotting a lie:

• Be **vigilant*** against warning signs. Take note of any strange behavior or warning signs that you may notice. Don't dismiss the possibility of a lie or overlook it. It is more likely that people will lie to you in the future if they know that they can **get away with*** it.

• Itching of the nose. Itching or rubbing of the nose can be a direct sign of an impending lie as cells release additional **histamine*** when a person is lying.

• Avoidance. Turning away from someone or looking away indicates an avoidance response. Speaking indirectly and separating of eye contact, or even looking away from someone entirely, can be a serious warning sign.

• **Evasive*** language. Phrases like "honestly" and "I swear" are designed to change or alter the perception of someone about actions. Repetitive use of this kind of evasive language suggests a strong desire to alter a situation and is a common trait of lying.

• Covering the senses. The covering or blocking of the eyes, ears or mouth and general acts of **aversion*** can indicate that someone is lying. These subtle actions are negative cues against whatever the person may be saying at the time.

1 Key Vocabulary

vigilant ***adj.*** carefully attentive

get away with ***idiom.*** to manage to do something bad without being punished or criticized for it

histamine ***n.*** a natural substance produced by the human immune system during allergic reactions

evasive ***adj.*** intentionally vague or ambiguous

aversion ***n.*** the act of turning yourself(or your gaze) away

2 Complete the blanks with the words from the box to form collocations with the italicized expressions.

lasting	dismissed	avoid	alter	cover

a. Establish personal connections with the audience. Audiences tend to distrust speakers who ____________ *eye contact.*

b. He *tried to* ____________ his embarrassment by starting to rub his hands together.

c. Unemployment has come down slightly but this does not ____________ *the fact that* it is still a major problem.

d. We don't usually *make a* ____________ *impression* when we're trying to do so.

e. The court ruled that Ms Hill had been *unfairly* ____________.

3 Are the following sentences true or false according to the text?

a. Itching or rubbing of the nose can be an indirect sign of an impending lie.

b. Speaking indirectly and separating of eye contact, or even looking away from someone entirely, can be a serious warning sign of an upcoming lie.

c. Some acts of aversion such as blocking the ears are positive cues for the truth of what the person is saying at the time.

4 Famous Quotes about Honesty and Lying

Q Of all feats of skill, the most difficult is that of being honest. — Comtesse Diane

Q The greatest advantage of speaking the truth is that you don't have to remember what you said. — Anonymous

Q Between a fellow who is stupid and honest and one who is smart and crooked, I will take the first. I won't get much out of him, but with that other guy I can't keep what I've got. — Lewis Hershey

Q There's one way to find out if a man is honest: ask him, if he says yes, you know he is crooked. — Mark Twain

Q Though I am not naturally honest, I am so sometimes by chance. — William Shakespeare

Q To make your children capable of honesty is the beginning of education. — John Ruskin

Q Any fool can tell the truth, but it requires a man of some sense to know how to lie well. — Samuel Butler

Q The liar's punishment is not in the least that he is not believed, but that he cannot believe anyone else. — George Bernard Shaw

Q I detest the man who hides one thing in the depth of his heart and speaks forth another. — Homer

Q Telling lies is a fault in a boy, an art in a lover, an accomplishment in a bachelor, and second-nature in a married man. — Helen Rowland

Q Without lies humanity would perish of despair and boredom. — Anatole France

Q Lying and stealing are next door neighbors. — Arabian proverb

Major schools of psychology

The study of psychology in a philosophical context dates back to the ancient civilizations of Egypt, Greece, China, India, and Persia. Historians note that Greek philosophers, including Thales, Plato, and Aristotle (especially in his *De Anima* treatise), covered the workings of the mind in their writings. As early as the 4th century BC, Greek physician Hippocrates theorized that mental disorders were of a physical, rather than divine, nature.

Structuralism

German physician Wilhelm Wundt is credited with introducing psychological discovery into a laboratory setting. Known as the "father of experimental psychology", he founded the first psychological laboratory, at Leipzig University, in 1879. Wundt focused on breaking down mental processes into the most basic components, motivated in part by an analogy to recent advances in chemistry, and its successful investigation of the elements and structure of material. Although Wundt, himself, was not a structuralist, his student Edward Titchener, a major figure in early American psychology, was a structuralist thinker opposed to functionalist approaches.

Functionalism

Functionalism formed as a reaction to the theories of the structuralist school of thought and was heavily influenced by the work of the American philosopher, scientist, and psychologist William James. James felt that psychology should have practical value, and that psychologists should find out how the mind can function to a person's benefit. In his book, *The Principles of Psychology*, published in 1890, he laid the foundations for many of the questions that psychologists would explore for years to come. Other major functionalist thinkers included John Dewey and Harvey Carr.

Other 19th-century contributors to the field include the German psychologist Hermann Ebbinghaus, a pioneer in the experimental study of memory, who developed quantitative models of learning and forgetting, and the

Russian-Soviet physiologist Ivan Pavlov, who discovered in dogs a learning process that was later termed "classical conditioning" and applied to human beings.

Starting in the 1950s, the experimental techniques developed by Wundt, James, Ebbinghaus, and others re-emerged as experimental psychology became increasingly cognitivist—concerned with information and its processing—and, eventually, constituted a part of the wider cognitive science. In its early years, this development was seen as a "revolution," as cognitive science both responded to and reacted against then-popular theories, including psychoanalytic and behaviorist theories.

Psychoanalysis

From the 1890s until his death in 1939, the Austrian physician Sigmund Freud developed psychoanalysis, which comprised a method of investigating the mind and interpreting experience; a systematized set of theories about human behavior; and a form of psychotherapy to treat psychological or emotional distress, especially unconscious conflict. Freud's psychoanalytic theory was largely based on interpretive methods, introspection and clinical observations. It became very well known, largely because it tackled subjects such as sexuality, **repression***, and the unconscious mind as general aspects of psychological development. These were largely considered taboo subjects at the time, and Freud provided a **catalyst*** for them to be openly discussed in polite society. Clinically, Freud helped to pioneer the method of free association and a therapeutic interest in dream interpretation.

Freud had a significant influence on Swiss psychiatrist Carl Jung, whose analytical psychology became an alternative form of depth psychology. Other well-known psychoanalytic scholars of the mid-20th century included Erik Erikson, Melanie Klein, D.W. Winnicott, Karen Horney, Erich Fromm, John Bowlby, and Sigmund Freud's daughter, Anna Freud. Throughout the 20th century, psychoanalysis evolved into diverse schools of thought, most of which may be classed as Neo-Freudian.

Psychoanalytic theory and therapy were criticized by psychologists such as Hans Eysenck, and by philosophers including Karl Popper. Popper, a philosopher of science, argued that psychoanalysis had been mis-represented as a scientific discipline, whereas Eysenck said that psychoanalytic **tenets*** had been contradicted by experimental data. By the end of 20th century, psychology departments in American universities had become scientifically oriented, marginalizing Freudian theory and dismissing it as a "**desiccated*** and dead" historical artifact. Meanwhile, however, researchers in the emerging field of neuro-psychoanalysis defended some of Freud's ideas on scientific grounds, while scholars of the humanities maintained that Freud was not a "scientist at all, but ... an interpreter."

Behaviorism

In the United States, behaviorism became the dominant school of thought during the 1950s. Behaviorism is a discipline that was established in the early 20th century by John B. Watson, and embraced and extended by Edward Thorndike, Clark L. Hull, Edward C. Tolman, and later B.F. Skinner. Theories of learning emphasized the ways in which people might be predisposed, or conditioned, by their environments to behave in certain ways.

Classical conditioning was an early behaviorist model. It posited that behavioral tendencies are determined by immediate associations between various environmental stimuli and the degree of pleasure or pain that follows. Behavioral patterns, then, were understood to consist of organisms' conditioned responses to the stimuli in their environment. The stimuli were held to exert influence in proportion to their prior repetition or to the previous intensity of their associated pain or pleasure. Much research consisted of laboratory-based animal experimentation, which was increasing in popularity as physiology grew more sophisticated.

Skinner's behaviorism shared with its **predecessors*** a philosophical inclination toward positivism and determinism. He believed that the contents of the mind were not open to scientific scrutiny and that scientific psychology should emphasize the study of observable behavior. He focused on behavior-environment relations and analyzed overt and covert(i.e., private) behavior as a function of the organism interacting with its environment. Behaviorists usually rejected or de-emphasized dualistic explanations such as "mind" or "consciousness"; and, in lieu of probing an "unconscious mind" that underlies unawareness, they spoke of the "contingency-shaped behaviors" in which unawareness becomes outwardly manifest.

Linguist Noam Chomsky's critique of the behaviorist model of language acquisition is widely regarded as a key factor in the decline of behaviorism's prominence. Martin Seligman and colleagues discovered that the conditioning of dogs led to outcomes that opposed the predictions of behaviorism. But Skinner's behaviorism did not die, perhaps in part because it generated successful practical applications.

Humanistic psychology

Humanistic psychology was developed in the 1950s in reaction to both behaviorism and psychoanalysis. By using phenomenology, inter-subjectivity, and first-person categories, the humanistic approach sought to glimpse the whole person—not just the fragmented parts of the personality or cognitive functioning. Humanism focused on fundamentally and uniquely human issues, such as individual free will, personal growth, self-actualization, self-identity, death, aloneness, freedom, and meaning. The humanistic approach was distinguished by its emphasis on subjective meaning, rejection of determinism, and concern for positive growth rather than pathology. Some of the founders of the humanistic school of thought were American psychologists Abraham Maslow, who formulated a hierarchy of human needs, and Carl Rogers, who created and developed client-centered therapy. Later, positive psychology opened up humanistic themes to scientific modes of exploration.

Gestalt

Wolfgang Kohler, Max Wertheimer and Kurt Koffka co-founded the school of Gestalt psychology. This approach is based upon the idea that individuals experience things as unified wholes. This approach to psychology began in Germany and Austria during the late 19th century in response to the **molecular*** approach of structuralism. Rather than breaking down thoughts and behavior to their smallest element, the Gestalt position maintains that the whole of experience is important, and the whole is different from the sum of its parts.

Existentialism

In the 1950s and 1960s, largely influenced by the work of German philosopher Martin Heidegger and Danish philosopher Soren Kierkegaard, psychoanalytically trained American psychologist Rollo May pioneered an existential branch of psychology, which included existential psychotherapy, a method of therapy that operates on the belief that inner conflict within a person is due to that individual's confrontation with the givens of existence.

Existential psychologists differed from others often classified as humanistic in their comparatively neutral view of human nature and in their relatively positive assessment of anxiety. Existential psychologists emphasized the humanistic themes of death, free will, and meaning, suggesting that meaning can be shaped by myths, or narrative patterns, and that it can be encouraged by an acceptance of the free will requisite to an authentic, albeit often anxious, regard for death and other future prospects.

Cognitivism

Cognitive psychology is the branch of psychology that studies mental processes including problem solving, perception, memory, and learning. As part of the larger field of cognitive science, this branch of psychology is related to other disciplines including neuroscience, philosophy, and linguistics. Noam Chomsky helped to launch a "cognitive revolution" in psychology when he criticized the behaviorists' notions of "stimulus", "response", and "reinforcement". Chomsky argued that such ideas—which Skinner had borrowed from animal experiments in the laboratory—could be applied to complex human behavior, most notably language acquisition, in only a superficial and vague manner. The postulation that humans are born with the instinct or "innate facility" for acquiring language posed a challenge to the behaviorist position that all behavior, including language, is **contingent*** upon learning and reinforcement.

Meanwhile, advances in technology helped to renew interest and belief in the mental states and representations—i.e., the cognition—that had fallen out of favor with behaviorists. English neuroscientist Charles Sherrington and Canadian psychologist Donald O. Hebb used experimental methods to link psychological phenomena with the structure and function of the brain. With the rise of computer science and artificial intelligence, analogies were drawn between the processing of information by humans and information processing by machines. Research in cognition had proven practical since World War II, when it aided in the understanding of weapons operation. By the late 20th century, though, cognitivism had become the dominant paradigm of psychology, and cognitive psychology emerged as a popular branch.

Assuming both that the covert mind should be studied, and that the scientific method should be used to study it, cognitive psychologists set such concepts as **subliminal*** processing and implicit memory in place of the psychoanalytic unconscious mind or the behavioristic contingency-shaped behaviors. Elements of behaviorism and cognitive psychology were synthesized to form the basis of cognitive behavioral therapy, a form of psychotherapy modified from techniques developed by American psychologist Albert Ellis and American psychiatrist Aaron T. Beck. Cognitive psychology was subsumed along with other disciplines, such as philosophy of mind, computer science, and neuroscience, under the cover discipline of cognitive science.

1 Key Vocabulary

repression ***n.*** the act of restraining painful or disturbing memories unconsciously from the conscious mind

catalyst ***n.*** a person or thing that causes a change

tenet ***n.*** an opinion, belief, or doctrine held as true by members of a profession, group, or movement

desiccated ***adj.*** lacking in spirit or vitality

predecessor ***n.*** a person who precedes another in time; something that indicates the approach of something or someone

molecular ***adj.*** pertaining to simple or basic organization or form

contingent ***adj.*** dependent upon certain conditions; something that may or may not happen; happening by chance

subliminal ***adj.*** below the level of consciousness; insufficient to produce conscious awareness but enough to provoke a response

2 Fill in the blank with an appropriate word from the words below.

divine	catalyst	reinforcement	artifact
humanistic	experimental	contingent	subsume

a. The performance at the Sylvan Theater received a lot of attention for its weird and ___________ aspects.
b. The completion of the merger is ___________ upon the satisfaction of certain conditions included in the merger agreement.
c. A Canadian woman returned an ancient ___________ to Italy, 50 years after taking it while on her honeymoon.
d. A degree of higher education does not mean you have a ___________ right to health, wealth, and happiness.
e. Video games have the potential to ___________ almost all other forms of entertainment media.
f. Experts say that the protest in the city of Ferguson could become as much of a ___________ of social changes.
g. Negative ___________ strengthens a behavioral response by taking away a negative outcome.
h. ___________ Education refers to an educational philosophy that believes we are, by nature, self-developing creatures.

3 Choose the school of psychology that the following study result has to do with.

psychoanalysis	behaviorism	cognitivism

If you take a toy duck and show it to a 12-month-old infant, then put your hand under a cushion, leave the duck there and bring your hand out, the child will only look in your hand, almost never under the cushion. At this age children behave as though things they can't see don't even exist. And yet, just six months later, a child will typically look under the cushion. It has learnt that things that are hidden from view can continue to exist.

4 What does it mean?

Your friend sent you a text message that she dreamt the following dream and was curious about what it meant, asking your help to interpret it.

> "I was digging through my back pack and found a bundle of cash and then started digging again. And I found a note saying "Good Luck!" Then I woke up."

How do you interpret it? Write down your interpretation below.

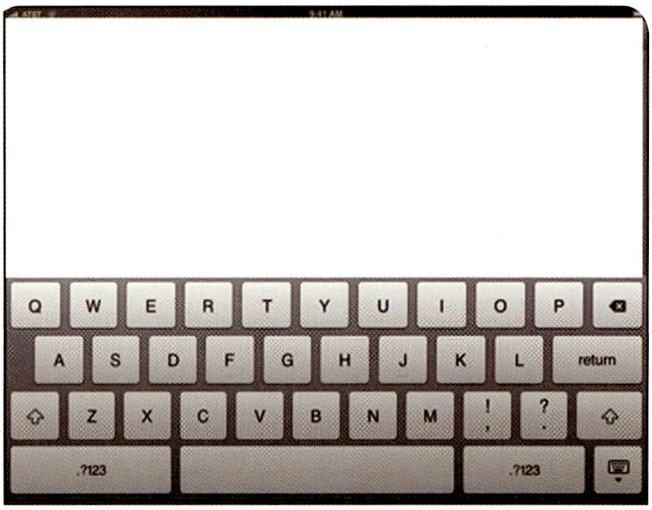

Cross-word puzzle(adjectives of feelings)

Across words

upset anxious delighted furious happy cheerful

Down words

surprised angry nervous depressed pleased proud scary

Pricing strategies

Consumer psychology and pricing

The cost of a product or service is relative to what the buyer thinks that cost should be. Based on his or her previous experiences, the customer will judge whether prices are too high, too low, or on target. Through personal experiences, advertising, and a base knowledge of standard pricing, customers will have a good idea of where your prices should fall in relation to the market and your competitors. By using psychology, you can present a perception of value or discount that will help you to sell your products. For example, the common use of $ 29.99 over $ 30.00 has long been a matter of pricing psychology that says: Although there is only a 1 cent difference, something in the 9 range is a greater bargain than something in the 10 range. In fact, studies show that odd numbers are more commonly associated with lower prices than even numbers. Giving an item free with purchase is primarily a perception of savings. While a buy-one-get-one-free offer represents a small savings to the customer, it draws more business because of the idea of getting something for free. Other factors that play into the perception of pricing include availability. If, for example, you indicate a one-day sale, the idea that availability is limited will encourage the customer to act quickly rather than **mull over*** the purchase. Likewise, if you know that supply and demand are in your favor, you can **stand by*** a higher price and let it be known that only a few items remain available. Limited items always appear as more valuable.

Reference price

People often compare a product's price to a "reference price" that they maintain in their minds for the product or product category in question. A "reference price" is the price that people expect or deem to be reasonable for a certain type of product. Several factors affect reference prices: Memory of past price; Frame of reference (compared to competitive prices, pre-sale prices, manufacturer's suggested prices, channel-specific prices, marked prices before discounts, substitute product prices, etc.).

Price quality inferences

Consumers often rely heavily on price as a predictor of quality and typically overestimate the strength of this relation. Furthermore, the inferences of quality they make on the basis of price can influence their actual purchase decisions. A bottle of perfume priced $ 500 might contain $ 50 worth of scent, but gift givers pay $ 500 to communicate their high **regard*** for the receiver.

Price Cues

A price cue is defined as any marketing tactic used to persuade customers that the company's prices offer good value compared to competitors' prices, past prices or future prices. The leading economic explanation for why price cues are effective focuses on the role of customer price knowledge and the ability of customers to evaluate whether prices offer good value. A common example of a price cue is placing a sign at the point of purchase claiming an item is on "Sale".

Geographical pricing

In this pricing the company decides how to price its product to different customers in different locations and countries.

a. Barter: The direct exchange of goods, with no money and no third party involved.
b. Compensation deal: The seller receives some percentage of the payment in cash and the rest in products. A British aircraft manufacturer sold planes to Brazil for 70 percent cash and the rest in coffee.
c. Buyback arrangement: The seller sells a plant, equipment, or technology to another country and agrees to accept as partial payment products manufactured with the supplied equipment. A U.S. Chemical company built a plant for an Indian company and accepted partial payment in cash and the remainder in chemicals manufactured at the plant.
d. Offset: The seller receives full payment in cash but agrees to spend a substantial amount of the money in that country within a stated time period. For example, PepsiCo sells its cola syrup to Russia for rubles and agrees to buy Russian vodka at a certain rate for sale in the United States.

Price discounts and allowances

Offering discounts can be a useful tactic in response to aggressive competition by a competitor. However, discounting can be dangerous unless carefully controlled and conceived as part of your overall marketing strategy. Discounting is common in many industries—in some it is so **endemic*** as to render normal price lists practically meaningless. This is not to say that there is anything particularly wrong with price discounting provided that you are getting something specific that you want in return.

Promotional Pricing

Companies can use several pricing techniques to stimulate early purchase.

a. Loss-leader pricing: Supermarkets and department stores often drop the price on well-known brands to stimulate additional store traffic. This pays if the revenue on the additional sales compensates for the lower margins on the loss-leader items. Manufacturers of loss-leader brands typically object because this practice can **dilute*** the brand image and bring complaints from retailers who charge the list price. Manufacturers have tried to restrain **intermediaries*** from loss-leader pricing through lobbying for retail-price-maintenance laws, but these laws have been revoked.

b. Special-event pricing: Sellers will establish special prices in certain seasons to draw in more customers.

c. Cash rebates: Auto companies and other consumer-goods companies offer cash rebates to encourage purchase of the manufacturers' products within a specified time period. Rebates can help clear inventories without cutting the stated list price.

d. Low-interest financing: Instead of cutting its price, the company can offer customers low-interest financing. Automakers have even announced no-interest financing to attract customers.

e. Longer payment terms: Sellers, especially mortgage banks and auto companies, stretch loans over longer periods and thus lower the monthly payments. Consumers often worry less about the cost (i.e., the interest rate) of a loan and more about whether they can afford the monthly payment.

f. Warranties and service contracts: Companies can promote sales by adding a free or low-cost warranty or service contract.

g. Psychological discounting: This strategy involves setting an artificially high price and then offering the product at substantial savings. Promotional-pricing strategies are often a zero-sum game.

Differentiated Pricing

Companies often adjust their basic price to accommodate differences in customers, products, locations, and so on.

a. Customer-segment pricing: Different customer groups are charged different prices for the same product or service. For example, museums often charge a lower admission fee to students and senior citizens.

Admission

$12 aduits(18+)

$9 senior citizens (65+)

$9 students with valid ID

$6 children (3-12)

Free for Museum members and children under 3

b. Product-form pricing: Different versions of the product are priced differently but not **proportionately*** to their respective costs.

c. Image pricing: Some companies price the same product two different levels based on image differences. A perfume manufacturer can put the perfume in one bottle, give it a name and image, and price it at $ 50. It can put the same perfume in another bottle with a different name and image and price it at $ 200.

d. Channel pricing: Coca-Cola carries a different price depending on whether it is purchased in a fine restaurant, a fast-food restaurant, or a vending machine.

e. Location pricing: The same product is priced differently at different locations even though the cost of offering at each location is the same. A theater varies its seat prices according to audience preferences for different locations.

f. Time pricing: Prices are varied by season, day, or hour. Public utilities vary energy rates to commercial users by time of day and weekend versus weekday. Restaurants charge less to "early bird" customers.

1 Key Vocabulary

mull over ***v.*** to consider something carefully
stand by ***v.*** to keep or maintain
regard ***n.*** affection, respect, or esteem
endemic ***adj.*** regularly found and very common among a particular group or in a particular area
dilute ***v.*** to reduce the strength, efficiency, or force of
intermediary ***n.*** a person who acts as a mediator or agent between persons
proportionately ***adv.*** to a corresponding size, degree, or extent

2 Complete the sentence with the correct form of the words in the box.

availability, deem, tactic, offset, revoke, inventory, accomodate

a. They used pressure __________ to force them to stop the strike, including cutting food and water supplies.
b. The historic theater was remodeled to __________ a variety of programming.
c. They are going to hold a big fire sale to liquidate their __________.
d. If you already know the date of your event, you can call her office and

check her ____________ to discuss the specifics of your meeting.

e. The advantages of the system were considered large enough to ____________ the inconvenience of regular consultation.

f. The judge ____________ his driver's license for multiple traffic offenses.

g. The superintendent will take whatever action she ____________ appropriate in the case.

3 Let's suppose you're a general manager of a large supermarket and want to attract more customers by using a loss-leader item. Create an advertising slogan for the item you would choose?

____

____

____

4 Grammar Focus

> Discounting is common in many industries—in some it is ***so endemic as to*** render normal price lists practically meaningless.

You often use a 'to' infinitive clause after 'so' followed by an adjective to express the result of an action or situation.

a. Sometimes she scolded herself so severely as to bring tears into her eyes.

b. I didn't think anyone would be so inconsiderate as to block my driveway.

c. Most of the people they care for are in step-down units, which means that they're not so ill as to need intensive care.

d. Would you be so kind as to remove your feet from my chair?

5 For each word in Group A, find the corresponding synonym in Group B and antonym in Group C.

Group A	Synonym	Antonym
a. substitute(adj.)		
b. claim(v.)		
c. endemic(adj.)		
d. dilute(v.)		
e. substantial(adj.)		
f. worry(v.)		
g. vary(v.)		

Group B. Synonym	Group C. Antonym
rife	meager
thin	constrict
alternative	soothe
diversify	irreplaceable
postulate	fortify
vex	sporadic
considerable	retract

6 Packaging Abbreviations

approx.	approximately	kg	kilogram
bkt(bast)	basket	lt(lgt)	light
bndl	bundle	mxd	mixed
ctn	carton	pc	piece
delic	delicious	pk/pkg	packed/package
dz(doz)	dozen	qual(qlty)	quality
ea	each	sdls	seedless
exfcy	extra fancy	try/celpk	tray/cell packed
incl/incldg	include/including	wrpd	wrapped
jbo	jumbo	wxd	waxed

7 Famous Quotes about Price

- **Q** Dictionary is the only place that success comes before work. Hard work is the price we must pay for success. I think you can accomplish anything if you're willing to pay the price. — Vince Lombardi
- **Q** We will make electricity so cheap that only the rich will burn candles. — Thomas A. Edison
- **Q** Nature cannot be tricked or cheated. She will give up to you the object of your struggles only after you have paid her price. — Napoleon Hill
- **Q** My favorite things in life don't cost any money. It's really clear that the most precious resource we all have is time. — Steve Jobs
- **Q** The price of inaction is far greater than the cost of making a mistake. — Meister Eckhart
- **Q** The price for finding happiness is directly and inversely related to the cost of being sad. — Unknown
- **Q** Reading is a discount ticket to everywhere. — Mary Schmich
- **Q** What is a cynic? A man who knows the price of everything and the value of nothing. — Oscar Wilde
- **Q** The bitterness of poor quality remains long after low pricing is forgotten! — Leon M. Cautillo

Chapter 4

Science and Technology

A mystery on the highway

The highway had been practically traffic-free until Charlie and Danny spotted some distance ahead what appeared to be an old turtle-back-type auto traveling very slowly. As they closed the distance between their vehicle and this **relic*** from the past, their discussion turned from their insurance work to the old car ahead of them. While the style of the auto indicated it to be decades old, it appeared to be in showroom condition, which evoked words of admiration from both Charlie and Danny. Because the car was traveling so slowly, the two men decided to pass it, but before doing so, slowed to better appreciate the beauty and **mint*** condition of the vehicle. As they did so, Charlie noticed a very large bright orange license plate with the year "1940" clearly printed on it. This was most unusual and probably illegal unless **provisions*** had been made for the antique car to be used in ceremonial parades.

1 Key Vocabulary

relic ***n.*** something that has survived from the past, such as an object or custom

mint ***adj.*** (of coins, postage stamps, etc.) in perfect condition as issued

provision ***n.*** an agreed arrangement; a rule or condition.

2 Collocation

condition n.

1) ***ADJ.*** *excellent, good, mint, perfect, bad, original*: Within 60 days, we are happy to exchange any item returned in its original condition. / *critical, serious, stable, mental, physical*: He was in a critical condition, fighting for his life. / *medical, chronic, incurable, rare*: Having a chronic condition doesn't necessarily mean an illness is critical or dangerous. / *favorable, good, ideal, optimum, adverse, awful, difficult, harsh, terrible*: Conditions are very favorable for starting a new business.

2) ***V.*** *live, work:* There are hundreds of families living in harsh conditions. / *exist, prevail, change, improve:* Poor housing condition prevails in the town. / *have, suffer from*: He has a serious heart condition. / *impose, accept, agree to, comply with, meet, satisfy, be subject to*: We told them that we couldn't meet that condition.

3) ***PREP.*** *in*: The house was old-fashioned and in bad condition. / *out of*: He was overweight and out of condition. / *under*: Most doctors and nurses live under stressful conditions. / *on*: We will lend you the money on condition that it is repaid within 12 months.

3 Grammar Focus

> While the style of the auto indicated it to be decades old, it appeared to be in showroom condition, ***which*** evoked words of admiration from both Charlie and Danny.

Sentential relative clauses say something about the whole situation described in the entire preceding clause, not just some noun phrase in it. They are punctuated with a comma or dash in front of them and introduced by *which*. In conversation, sentential relative clauses can be added by a second speaker.

a. Small computers need only small amounts of power, *which* means that they will run on small batteries.

b. He kept on bragging about his success, *which* annoyed all of us.

c. A: She skips at least one meal a day.

   B: *Which* is not good.

   A: Yeah.

Where do you keep your laboratory?

Einstein's office at Princeton

Albert Einstein was a world **cult*** figure long before he came to the Institute for Advanced Study. When in 1919 astronomers confirmed his prediction that light rays would be bent by the sun's gravity, people went crazy. They named babies and cigars after him. The London Palladium offered him a three-week stand, asking him to name his own price. Two German professors made a "relativity film" and showed it on both sides of the Atlantic. When Einstein entered the home of J.B.S. Haldane to stay the night, Haldane's daughter took one look at the man and promptly fainted dead away. The press **hailed*** Einstein's theories as the greatest achievement in the history of human thought, and Einstein himself as the greatest man who ever lived.

He was, after all, the messenger of the new order. Light was weight, space is **warped***, and the universe has four dimensions. People loved it. They didn't know what any of it meant, of course, but that didn't matter. Einstein did. He was the man who invented it all, who understood it. He became their hero, the new messiah, the First Knowledgian and Supreme Head of the Vast Physical Universe.

Einstein was **revered*** as a god, but the man himself was the essence of modesty and kindliness, and he never understood why people made such a fuss. He, at least, treated others democratically, as equals: "I speak to everyone in the same way," he said, "whether he is the garbage man or the President of the University." Of course, if you were **single-minded*** about it you would find some ... exceptions, as for example the time he sent a paper to the *Physical Review*, and the editor dared to return it for revisions. *Well!* The poor editor had only done his job, sending Einstein's article—the same as he would anyone else's—to outside referees for evaluation. But this was not acceptable to Albert Einstein, who never sent one of his articles *there* again. But what does this prove? Only that the greatest physicist the world has ever known had, after all, an ego. If there's anything that most of the Institute's so-called **prima donas*** of science share, it's a healthy and well-developed ego.

In the world of ordinary men, Einstein may have been the humble genius who never wore socks (at least he wore shoes), but up there in the Platonic Heaven it was something else again. The man had this absolutely incredible **hubris***. He thought he might be able to understand the plan of the entire universe—the whole thing, from the largest galaxy to the smallest quark. He thought he could comprehend it all, that he could find a single overarching set of principles that would cover *everything*, in a theory of the unified field. And how would he do this but by theorizing, in the best Platonic-heavenly tradition. While the cyclotron people smashed their atoms to the Kingdom of God, while astronomers aimed their gigantic telescopes across billions of frigid light years, Einstein would close himself off in a room, pull the shades down, and as he used to say, "I will a little think." He'd scribble out a few equations, make a few mental **jottings***, and lo and behold pretty soon he'd figure it all out. Just by thinking ... no machines or instruments for him. Someone once asked the great physicist where he kept his laboratory. Einstein smiled and took a fountain pen out of his pocket. "Here," he said.

1 Key Vocabulary

cult ***n.*** 1. religious group, especially one with beliefs that most people consider strange or dangerous
2. extreme admiration for someone or something
3. someone or something that a particular group of people are very enthusiastic about but that most people do not like or know about

hail ***v.*** 1. If it hails, small hard balls of ice fall from the sky like rain.
2. to say publicly how good or important someone or something is; greet enthusiastically

warp ***v.*** 1. to make or become twisted out of shape: *The door has been warped by all the rain we've had lately.*
2. to cause to think or act in an abnormal way: *His experiences had warped his judgement.*

revere ***v.*** to regard with feelings of respect

single-minded ***adj.*** having but one aim or purpose; determined

prima dona ***n.*** 1. the most important female singer in an opera
2. someone who thinks that they are very important or special, and who is very difficult to please

hubris ***n.*** being very proud and believing in your own importance

jotting ***n.*** a brief note

2 Find these sentences in the passage. Who or what does the underlined expression refer to?

Haldane's daughter took one look at **the man** and promptly fainted dead away.	
They didn't know what any of **it** meant, of course, but **that** didn't matter.	
But **this** was not acceptable to Albert Einstein, who never sent one of his articles ***there*** again.	
He thought he could comprehend **it** all ...	

3 Correct the sentence which is NOT true of the passage.

a. When in 1919 astronomers confirmed Einstein's prediction that light rays would be bent by the sun's gravity, people got furious.

b. The London Palladium offered Einstein a three-week stand, asking him to name his own price.
c. Einstein was revered as a god, but the man himself was the essence of modesty and kindliness, and he understood why people made such a fuss.
d. Einstein would close himself off in a room, pull the shades down, and as he used to say, "I will a little think."

4 Famous Quotes about Genius

Q To sentence a man of true genius to the drudgery of a school is to put a racehorse in a mill. — Charles Caleb

Q Improvement makes straight roads; but the crooked roads without improvement are roads of genius. — William Blake

Q Results! Why, man, I have gotten a lot of results. I know several thousand things that won't work. — Thomas A. Edison

Q Genius is one of the many forms of insanity. — Cesare Lombroso

Q Men of genius are meteors intended to burn to light their century. — Napoléon

Q Doing easily what others find difficult is talent; doing what is impossible for talent is genius. — Henri Frederic Amiel

Q Thousands of geniuses live and die undiscovered either by themselves or by others. — Unknown

Q Everyone has a talent. What is rare is the courage to follow the talent to the dark place where it leads. — Erica Jong

Q Genius is entitled to respect only when it promotes the peace and improves the happiness of mankind. — Robert Devereux Essex

Learning from nature

In 1941, a Swiss engineer named George de Mestral returned from a hunting trip with seeds clinging to his pants and tangled in his dog's fur. When de Mestral examined the seeds under a microscope, he marveled at how they **bristled*** with hooks **ingeniously*** shaped to grasp at animal fur. "Most people stop at the 'Oh, that's cool, that's what nature does,'" says Janine Benyus. "He probably had to go back a lot of times," she adds, "and really look" at those hooks. A seed, of course, can clamp onto wool socks with surprising force, and—even more amazing—once you **pry*** it off, it can stick again and again, like glue that never wears out. But how to imitate this trick with human-made stuff? Eventually de Mestral learned to mold nylon into a fabric **studded*** with tiny hooks or loops that acted like artificial seeds.

When Velcro first arrived in America, it caused a sensation. In 1958, a financial columnist named Sylvia Porter announced that "a new fastening device" had so **bewitched*** her that she spent days playing with it. "It's on my desk as I type this," she wrote. As for Benyus, she hopes our future will be held together with detachable hooks. **Myriad*** plants and animals use Velcro-like attachments, she says, and engineers are now studying nature to learn how to create a "super-Velcro" that would be strong enough to join the pieces of a computer or maybe even a car. She points out that super-Velcro offers a lesson in sustainability. "If we were able to put the parts of a computer together with super-Velcro, we could send the computer back to the manufacturer, and they could disassemble it and reuse different parts or recycle it easier." Benyus says. "Glue actually contaminates recyclables. We throw things in a landfill just because they're glued together. Instead, we should take our machines apart and use the building blocks again." The term Velcro is now commonly used to mean any type of hook and loop fastener, but remains a registered trademark in many countries used by the Velcro company to distinguish their brand of fasteners from their competitors.

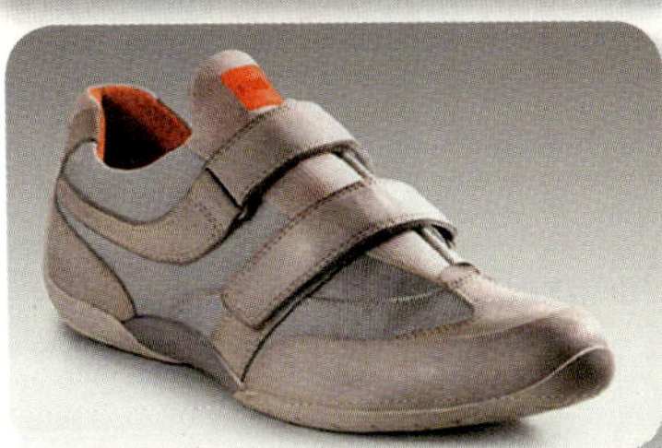

Various Uses of Velcro

1 Key Vocabulary

bristle ***v.*** to stand like a stiff hair
ingeniously ***adv.*** in a brilliant manner
pry ***v.*** to extract, detach, or open with difficulty
stud ***v.*** to cover or furnish
bewitch ***v.*** to attract someone a lot
myriad ***adj.*** too numerous to be counted

hair brush with bristles

2 What kind of invention is the sentence about? Choose the relevant one from the list.

washing machine, microscope, eraser, sprinkler, hair dryer, credit card, TV remote control, thermometer

a. Don't smoke under or near me. If you do, I am going to soak you up like a sponge.
b. If you let the sun shine on my cheeks, my face will get blushed.
c. I just keep going round and round and never get anywhere.
d. Countless people can get their hands on items whether they can afford them or not. They just ask me to come out of the wallet.
e. Why are you so worried about making mistakes? You don't have to. I will go and cover them so no one can notify them.
f. Don't place or store me where it can fall or be pulled into a tub or sink. You may be electrocuted.
g. Things grow larger and bigger under my eyeglasses.
h. People all over the world like to stay close to me, and they even want to hold me on their hands.

3 Describe some features of an invention you wish existed.

Chapter 5

Business

Undercover marketing, is it ethical?

Undercover* marketing seeks to influence buying decisions without tipping off the consumer about the manipulation. Also labeled buzz, guerrilla marketing or stealth marketing, these tactics take four distinct forms. Ad spies and leaners are actors hired to get people buying or discussing featured products. Advertising agencies also get messages across through product placement or video releases, which mimic conventional broadcast reports. These trends worry critics, who describe undercover marketing as manipulative and **deceptive***.

Ad Spies

Paying actors to secretly **pitch*** products is a favorite tactic of undercover marketers. Ad spies are often hired to talk up local products to help spread a client's market share. For example, a major food company which sought to develop a new healthy snack featured ad spies hanging around clinics as they **sampled*** the new product.

Leaners

"Leaners," as they are nicknamed, represent a **ramped up*** variation on the ad spy approaches. Companies using this method send their products with actors to trendy establishments, where they strike up conversations with total strangers. However, the conversations follow a scripted format designed to get customers to interact with the product in some way. One

technique involves having an actor's phone ring at the bar, followed by the caller's picture popping up onscreen. Critics call the practice deceptive, since the actors never identify themselves, nor reveal their true purpose.

Product Placements

Prominently displaying products is standard practice in film and TV production. Undercover marketers are also exploiting this method of product placement to their advantage. A beer company followed this logic in placing 50,000 bottle caps bearing its name in bars during Mardi Gras and spring break celebrations. In another scenario, a Massachusetts firm sent fake riders onto local subways with newspapers that contained equally **phony*** back page ads for its products. By doing so, the company hoped to convince people that it was well-established and successful.

Video News Releases(VNR)

For critics, video news releases represent a significant blurring of boundaries between journalism and marketing—since the publicists who appear in them are **passed off*** as traditional broadcast reporters. However, although styled like news reports, VNRs focus on selling a product. Local TV stations often respond by inserting their own graphics, or hiring a staff reporter to re-dub the script in their voice. This approach further disguises a station's relationship with its client, while making the finished product sound like one of its own reports.

1 Key Vocabulary

undercover ***adj.*** acting in secret
deceptive ***adj.*** likely or designed to mislead; causing one to believe what is not true or fail to believe what is true
pitch ***v.*** to attempt to promote or sell
sample ***v.*** to taste a small amount of food or drink to decide whether you like it
ramp up ***v.*** to increase or strengthen
phony ***adj.*** not real; intended to deceive
pass off ***v.*** to give a false identity

2 **What kind of product/service do you think the following advertising slogan is for? Choose the relevant one from the list.**

a. Life is a journey. Enjoy the ride.
b. Cleans your teeth while it cleans your breath.
c. Making the sky the best place on earth.
d. Tastes as good as it smells.
e. Buy a bucket of chicken and have a barrel of fun.
f. It tastes like a chocolate milkshake, only crunchy!
g. You are in a beauty contest every day of your life.
h. Effortlessly cleaning out that dirty mouth of yours, so no one will ever know how bad your breath really was.
i. Give your baby something you never had as a baby. A drier bottom.

airline(Air France)

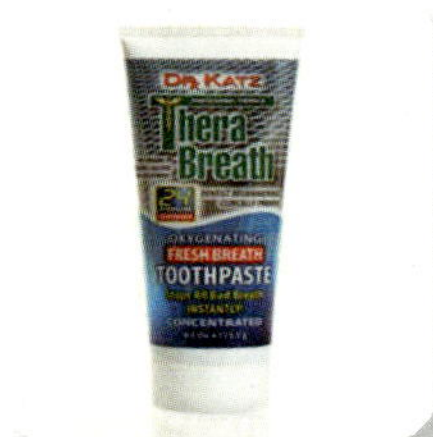

toothpaste(TheraBreath)

coffee(Maxwell House)

cereal(Cocoa Krispies)

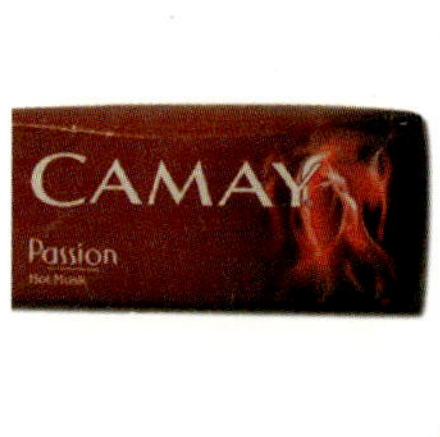

soap(Camay)

fast food(KFC)

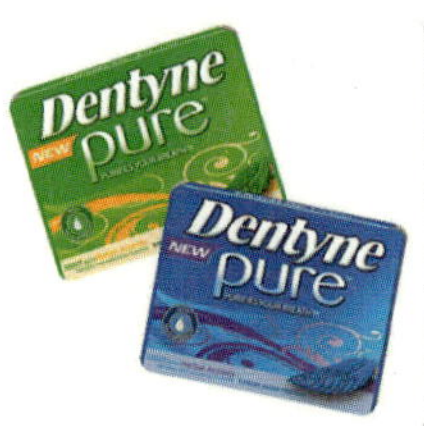

gum(Dentyne)

diaper(Pampers)

car(Nissan)

Starbucks marketing strategies

Every business can learn from another, especially if a particular business is one that has displayed tremendous success over the years. The Starbucks Corporation and its successful marketing strategies are definitely something that anyone interested in business can learn about. What sort of techniques did the company use, and how were these able to reach out and attract millions of people worldwide? Some of their best strategies are outlined below.

"Perfect Cup of Coffee"—Starbucks history has shown that they place a huge emphasis on product quality. Their coffee, even if priced slightly more expensive than expected, is notorious for satisfying customers with its rich, delicious taste and aroma.

"Third Place"—From the very beginning, the Starbucks marketing strategy has focused on creating the "third place" for everyone to go to between home and work. Creating this unique and relaxing "experience" and "atmosphere" for people has been very important for the company as they have realized that this is one of the strongest concepts attached to the company, to which customers have been strongly attracted.

"Customer Satisfaction"—Customer satisfaction is a very important issue with Starbucks. From entrance to the store to the very last drop of their coffees, it is a **must*** that customers feel the uniqueness of enjoying their Starbucks coffee experience. Without a doubt, Starbucks Coffee Company knows the answer to the question, "Why is customer service important?"

"Creating a Starbucks Community"—The Starbucks marketing strategy has even expanded to create a community around their brand. On their website, individuals are encouraged to express their experiences with Starbucks history, and the company strives to "personally" join in the discussions.

"Smart Partnerships"—Starbucks Coffee Company has been known to create strategic partnerships that demonstrate the fact that another way to grow your business is to partner smart. Over the years, the Starbucks Corporation has greatly increased sales just by using this strategy.

"Innovation"—Through the years, the Starbucks Coffee Company has been known to think up creative and innovative ideas to add to their products or services. They've added different flavors to their coffee, more food on their menu, and even became one of the firsts to offer internet capability in their stores.

"Brand Marketing"—The Starbucks marketing strategy has always focused on "**word-of-mouth***" advertising and letting the high quality of their products and services speak for themselves. For years, this has been uniquely Starbucks, and it has played a huge part in making Starbucks Coffee Company a success. The definition of **viral*** marketing speaks to this new word of mouth that Starbucks has run with, and made their own.

(Source: http://www.headstandmedia.com/images/history-of-starbucks-logo.jpg)

1 Key Vocabulary

must ***n.*** something that is absolutely required
word-of-mouth ***adj.*** expressed orally
viral ***adj.*** relating to or caused by a virus; very popular and spreading very quickly, especially on the Internet

2 Which marketing strategy does each sentence refer to?

Perfect Cup of Coffee, Third Place, Innovation, Brand Marketing

a. The Starbucks Coffee Company has focused on creating a space for everyone to go to between home and work.

b. The Starbucks Coffee Company has added different flavors to their coffee, more choices on their menu, and even became one of the firsts to offer internet capability in their stores.

c. An enormous emphasis on product quality has been placed even if their coffee is priced slightly more expensive than expected.

d. They have always focused on "word-of-mouth" advertising and letting the high quality of their products and services speak for themselves.

3 For each word in Group A, find the corresponding synonym in Group B and antonym in Group C.

Group A	Synonym	Antonym
a. definite		
b. satisfying		
c. uniqueness		
d. encourage		
e. grow		
f. capability		

Group B. Synonym	Group C. Antonym
singularity	insufficient
explicit	depress
expand	vague
adequate	incompetence
potential	diminish
boost	unoriginality

4 Marketing Terms & Concepts

Ad Copy: The printed text or spoken words in an advertisement.

Advertising Elasticity: The relationship between a change in advertising budget and the resulting change in product sales.

Brand: A name, term, design, symbol, or any other feature that identifies one seller's good or service as distinct from those of other sellers. The legal term for brand is trademark.

Counter Advertising: Advertising that takes a position contrary to an advertising message that preceded it. Such advertising may be used to take an opposing position on a controversial topic, or to counter an impression that might be made by another party's advertising.

End-User: The person who actually uses a product, whether or not they are the one who purchased the product.

Focus Group Interview: A research method that brings together a small group of consumers to discuss the product or advertising, under the guidance of a trained interviewer.

Infomercial: A commercial that is very similar in appearance to a news program, talk show, or other non-advertising program content.

Jingle: A short song, usually mentioning a brand or product benefit, used in a commercial.

Marketing Mix: The levels and interplay of the elements of a product's or service's marketing efforts, including product features, pricing, packaging, advertising, merchandising, distribution, and marketing budget.

Penetrated Market: Actual set of users actually consuming the product or service.

PPC(Pay Per Click): An internet advertising method in which the advertiser pays based solely on quality clicks.

Tag Line: A slogan or phrase that visually conveys the most important product attribute or benefit that the advertiser wishes to convey.

Vehicle: A specific channel or publication for carrying the advertising message to a target audience.

Wear Out: The point reached when an advertising campaign loses its effectiveness due to repeated overplay of ads.

Bowling alley wedding: How creativity is priceless in a bad economy

It wasn't the dream wedding Rachel Sifuentes, 28, **envisioned*** as a little girl. No walking down a church aisle. No DJ at the reception. No white dress. Instead, Sifuentes and her husband followed their attendants dancing down the center lane of a bowling alley where the neatly lined-up pins faded into the background. The ladies didn't carry flowers, but waved long ribbons. The bridal party relied on an iPod for entertainment. The bride wore a silky deep-blue gown—the groom's favorite color—purchased at a discount.

"Luckily, everything turned out to be great," said Sifuentes, who lives in Chicago, Illinois, and wanted to save money because her salary at the law firm where she works had been reduced. Sifuentes' bowling alley wedding in January may not have been traditional, but the creative ceremony saved her thousands of dollars at a time when wallet tightening has become necessary for many American families. Her **offbeat*** wedding is representative of a growing trend, wedding experts say, as brides are discovering cheap can be chic, and also inspire innovative party ideas. "Necessity breeds ingenuity," said Ariel Meadow Stallings, a writer who runs the online bridal site

Offbeat Bride. She explains what has **ushered*** in the recent trend of frugal yet creative brides: "It's the combination of the economy with the fact that through the '90s, there was a big explosion of the wedding industrial complex."

Weddings remain a multibillion-dollar industry and summer is the busiest season. There were about 2.2 million weddings in 2009, with each event averaging 128 guests, according to The Wedding Report Inc., a research company that tracks the wedding industry. But the wedding business may slowly be **eroding*** in the fragile economy. The average cost for a wedding dipped in 2009 to about $19,500 from a peak of $28,700 in 2007, said The Wedding Report Inc. So far this year, wedding spending has improved—with the economy—to an average of $23,800.

Sifuentes' bowling alley wedding was a bargain: She spent about $5,000, which included the ceremony and reception. Websites and blogs—such as A Practical Wedding and 2,000 Dollar Wedding—have surfaced over the last few years to help brides creatively **pinch their pennies***. In Maine this summer, one bride substituted a baked potato bar for a traditional five-course meal at the reception. Other brides have replaced costly gourmet cakes from bakeries with homemade Rice Krispies treats and chocolate chip cookies. Some couples recommended switching from a dinnertime reception to a brunch or hosting the wedding on a weekday night rather than on the more popular Saturday. Other brides have abandoned expensive **venues*** such as private hotels or banquet halls for public buildings, parks and libraries. One New York bride spent less than $600 on her wedding in 2007 by keeping the guest list short and having the ceremony in a public library.

When it comes to invitations, place settings, decorations and dresses, the brides have learned the power of DIY, which stands for "do it yourself." But it's not always easy to have an offbeat wedding. Some wedding experts caution the bride may not have enough time to handle the extra responsibilities. Other brides say they still feel families and friends expect them to throw a **lavish***, traditional wedding. "There was so much pressure on everything," said former bride Meg Keene, founder of the blog A Practical Wedding. "Everything was presented as obviously this is the option you'll choose, if you want it to be a good wedding."

For Sifuentes, throwing a bowling alley wedding came with some hesitation. She worried about what some guests would think about her cutbacks. "I was concerned that I was going to come off as a cheap bride or not having a very nice wedding," she said. "I didn't want it to be a **tacky*** wedding." But her bowling alley wedding turned out to be classy, she said. About 70 of the couple's closest friends and family members joined them to feast on an Italian buffet. There was plenty of dancing, but they also found time to bowl.

A Brides.com survey in 2009 also found brides are watching expenses. Four out of five couples set a budget for their wedding. Half the brides will spend time researching financing for the ceremony and reception, the survey said. "People are being smarter," said Ali Phillips, owner of a wedding planning boutique firm, Engaging Events by Ali, in Chicago. "They are asking themselves: Do we really need to have the fancy chairs? Do you really have to give wedding favors?"

Phillips, who has been a wedding consultant for nine years, said she noticed clients making cutbacks to guest lists and choosing fewer upgrades this year. For example, five years ago, the average guest list contained about 180 people. This year, the guest lists have about 120 people. Jennifer Crawford, 30, of Huntington Beach, California, kept her wedding budget a priority. At her wedding in April, she shaved costs by having a **seamstress*** copy the style of her dream gown that retailed at $2,800 at a boutique. Her handmade replica was a fraction of the cost—$650. "What was best about this idea was being personally involved in the design process," Crawford said. "I did not want a **cookie-cutter*** dress. I wanted it to be special and fun." In Oklahoma, bride-to-be Ashley Heckathorn, 24, estimated she will save up to $15,000 by making her own bouquets, which will save her from **whittling*** down the guest list. She is relying on Craigslist and friends' talents to find deals for her wedding.

Some wedding experts say the wedding industry is recovering. Xochitl Gonzalez, a wedding consultant at Always a Bridesmaid in New York, said her guests aren't as afraid to spend money on the ceremony and reception as they were when the economy initially plummeted. Rebecca Dolgin, executive editor at The Knot.com, said weddings are recession proof. But Dolgin said she noticed brides are shopping more carefully and comparing deals for their weddings. "People generally only get married once," Dolgin said. "There may be **ebbs and flows*** in the economy, but they are always going to look back on their wedding day."

1 Key Vocabulary

envision ***v.*** to picture in the mind; imagine
offbeat ***adj.*** unusual; unconventional
usher ***v.*** to introduce; to bring in
erode ***v.*** to wear down; to break up; to destroy gradually
pinch one's pennies ***idiom.*** to live economically
venue ***n.*** the place where some action takes place
lavish ***adj.*** spending, giving, or using more than necessary or reasonable
tacky ***adj.*** of cheap quality or in bad style
seamstress ***n.*** a woman who is expert at sewing, especially one who makes her living by sewing
cookie-cutter ***adj.*** appearing to be mass-produced by a tool to cut out cookie/biscuit dough in a particular shape
whittle ***v.*** to reduce or eliminate gradually
ebbs and flows ***n.*** declines and continuous progresses

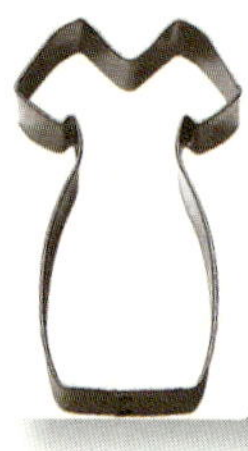

2 Find the word from the passage which matches each definition.

a. a narrow street with walls on both sides; a straight narrow course or track: __________

b. a gradual change or development that produces a particular result; the popular taste at a given time: __________

c. easily broken or damaged; lacking significance: __________

d. a ceremonial meal for many people, usually followed by speeches in honor of someone: __________

e. a reduction in quantity or rate, especially one made to save money: __________

f. something that you do for someone to help them; a small gift given to guests at a party: __________

3 Which of the following is NOT true according to the passage?

a. Sifuentes, who had a bowling alley wedding, wanted to save money because her salary at the law firm where she works had been reduced.

b. Weddings remain a multibillion-dollar industry and spring is the busiest season.

c. For Sifuentes, throwing a bowling alley wedding came with no hesitation and her wedding turned out to be classy.

d. Phillips, a wedding consultant, noticed clients making cutbacks to guest lists and choosing fewer upgrades this year.

e. Some wedding experts say the wedding industry is recovering.

4 Famous Quotes about Wedding and Marriage

Q The most dangerous food a man can eat is wedding cake. — Unknown

Q The woman cries before the wedding and the man after. — Polish proverb

Q A wedding is just like a funeral except that you get to smell your own flowers. — Grace Hansen

Q I dreamed of a wedding of elaborate elegance; a church filled with flowers and friends. I asked him what kind of wedding he wished for; he said one that would make me his wife. — Unknown

Q Who of us is mature enough for offspring before the offspring themselves arrive? The value of marriage is not that adults produce children but that children produce adults. — Peter de Vries

Q The general rule is that people who enjoy life also enjoy marriage. — Phyllis Battelle

Q I think men who have a pierced ear are better prepared for marriage. They've experienced pain and bought jewelry. — Rita Rudner

Q Often the difference between a successful marriage and a mediocre one consists of leaving about three or four things a day unsaid. — Harlan Miller

Q A successful marriage requires falling in love many times, always with the same person. — Mignon McLaughlin

Q Love is the dawn of marriage, and marriage is the sunset of love. — French proverb

5 A Wedding Invitation Card (Source: www.samplewords.com)

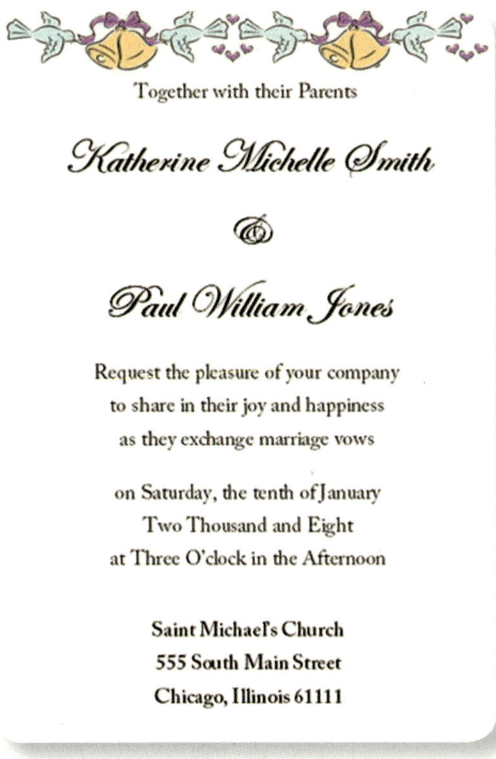

Together with their Parents

Katherine Michelle Smith

&

Paul William Jones

Request the pleasure of your company
to share in their joy and happiness
as they exchange marriage vows

on Saturday, the tenth of January
Two Thousand and Eight
at Three O'clock in the Afternoon

Saint Michael's Church
555 South Main Street
Chicago, Illinois 61111

Chapter 6

Politics

Academic turns city into a social experiment

Antanas Mockus had just resigned from the top job of Colombian National University. A mathematician and philosopher, Mockus looked around for another big challenge and found it: to be in charge of, as he describes it, "a 6.5 million person classroom." Mockus, who had no political experience, ran for mayor of Bogotá ; he was successful mainly because people in Colombia's capital city saw him as an honest guy. With an educator's inventiveness, Mockus turned Bogotá into a social experiment just as the city was choked with violence, lawless traffic, corruption, and gangs of street children who mugged and stole. It was a city perceived by some to be on the **verge*** of chaos.

People were desperate for a change, for a moral leader of some sort. The **eccentric*** Mockus, who communicates through symbols, humor, and metaphors, filled the role. When many hated the disordered city of Bogotá, he wore a Superman costume and acted as a superhero called "Supercitizen." People laughed at Mockus's **antics***, but the laughter began to break the ice of their extreme skepticism.

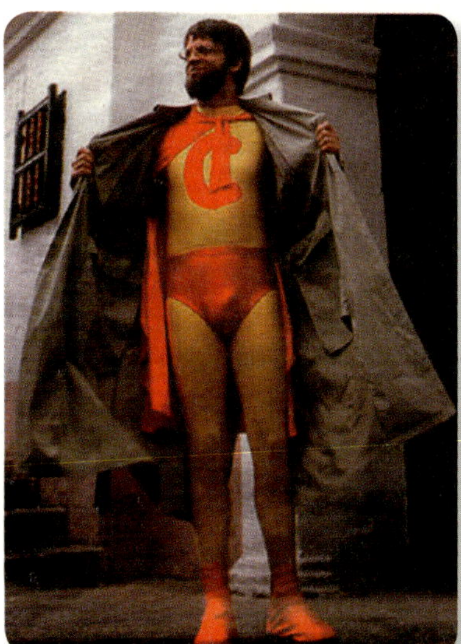

Mockus, the only son of a Lithuanian artist, burst onto the Colombian political scene in 1993 when, faced with a **rowdy*** auditorium of the school of arts' students, he dropped his pants and **mooned*** them to gain quiet. The gesture, he said at the time, should be understood "as a part of the resources which an artist can use." He resigned as **rector***, the top job of Colombian National University, and soon decided to run for mayor. The fact that he was seen as an unusual leader gave the new mayor the opportunity to try extraordinary things, such as having 420 mimes control traffic in Bogotá's chaotic and dangerous streets. He had the performers follow and mock pedestrians who didn't follow crosswalk rules. He launched a "Night for Women" and asked the city's men to stay home in the evening and care for the children; 700,000 women went out on the first of three nights that Mockus dedicated to them. When there was a water shortage, Mockus appeared on TV programs taking a shower and turning off the water as he soaped, asking his fellow citizens to do the same. In just two months people were using 14 percent less water, a savings that increased when people realized how much money they were also saving because of economic incentives approved by Mockus; water use is now 40 percent less than before the shortage. Here are a few more innovations from Antanas Mockus's two mayoral terms:

• Mockus mobilized people to protest against violence and terrorist attacks. He invented a "vaccine against violence," asking people to draw the faces of the people who had hurt them on balloons, which they then popped. About 50,000 people participated in this campaign.

• Mockus also embraced the concept of community policing. He tried to bring the community and the police closer together through the creation of Schools of Civic Security and local security fronts. In 2003, there were about 7,000 local security fronts in Bogotá. "It is very important to understand that the Schools and Fronts respond to a civic ideal. They have nothing to do with firearms but basically promote community organization," Mockus points out.

• Voluntary **disarmament*** days were held in December 1996 and again in 2003. Though less than 1 percent of the firearms in the city were given up, **homicides*** fell by 26 percent, thanks in part to the attention given to the program by the media. The percentage of people who think that it is better to have firearms in order to protect themselves fell from 24.8 percent in 2001 to 10.4 percent in 2003.

• In 2003, the Mockus administration provided 1,235,000 homes with **sewage*** service and 1,316,500 with water services. The city's provision of drinking water rose from 78.7 percent of homes in 1993 to 100 percent in 2003. The sewage service rose from 70.8 percent of homes in 1993 to 94.9 percent in 2003.

• When Mockus assumed power, many city positions were distributed according to council members' recommendations. "I stopped that, and some called me an anti-patronage fundamentalist," Mockus said. He remembers that when he handed a text explaining his goals of **transparency*** to one key council member, the council member first smiled, but later resigned.

1 Key Vocabulary

verge ***n.*** the edge or border of something
eccentric ***adj.*** departing from convention; unusual; odd
antic ***n.*** an attention-drawing funny or silly act
rowdy ***adj.*** disorderly; loud and rough; disturbing the public peace
moon ***v.*** to expose one's buttocks to others as a disrespectful gesture
rector ***n.*** the head of a university, school or college
disarmament ***n.*** the act of taking away or giving up weapons
homicide ***n.*** the killing of a human being by another person
sewage ***n.*** the system of carrying away waste water and human waste from houses and other buildings through large underground pipes or passages
transparency ***n.*** the quality of being clear

2 Vocabulary Expansion

Complete the following table with the appropriate words. The word-formation may not be the same for all of them.

noun	*adjective*	*person*	*verb*
	distributive distributable	distributor	
attention	attentive		
approval			approve
		skeptic	skepticize

3 Choose three statements which are true according to the passage.

a. Before he ran for mayor of Bogotá, Mockus had no political experience.
b. People laughed at Mockus's funny acts, but the laughter began to break the ice of their extreme positivism.
c. Mockus invented a "vaccine against violence," asking people to draw the faces of the people who had hurt them on balloons, which they then popped.
d. When there was a water shortage, Mockus hired mimes to appear on TV programs and to take a shower and turn off the water as they soaped.
e. Voluntary disarmament days were held in 1996 and again in 2003. Though less than 1 percent of the firearms in the city were given up, homicides fell by 26 percent, thanks solely to the establishment of the disarmament day.
f. The city's provision of drinking water rose from 70.8 percent of homes in 1993 to 94.9 percent in 2003.
g. When Mockus handed a text explaining his goals of transparency to one key council member, the council member resigned because he was not clear.

4 Grammar Focus

- He **had** 420 mimes **control** traffic in Bogotá's chaotic streets.
- He **had** the performers **follow** and **mock** pedestrians who didn't follow crosswalk rules.
- Many restaurants **let** women **have** discounted food and drinks.
- Many universities in the United States **have had** him **teach** people about his ideas.

vs.

- He **got** people **to trust** him because he was honest and had creative ideas.
- He **encouraged** people **to do** the same.
- He **got** citizens **to save** water and money.

Causative verbs such as *have, let,* and *make* are followed by the base form of a verb when you are telling someone to do something or to allow somebody to do it. Other common causative verbs including *get*, *encourage*, *allow*, *permit*, *convince*, and *force* are followed by to-infinitive forms.

HUMOR

A Senator, a clergyman, and a Boy Scout were passengers in a small plane that developed engine trouble. The pilot announced, "We'll have to bail out. Unfortunately, there are only three parachutes. I have a wife and seven small children. My family needs me. I'm taking one of the parachutes and jumping out!" And he jumped. Then the Senator said, "I am the smartest politician in the world. The country needs me. I'm taking one of the parachutes." And he jumped. The clergyman said to the Boy Scout, "I've had a good life and yours is still ahead of you. You take the last parachute." The youth shrugged and said, "Don't need to. There are two parachutes left. The smartest politician in the world just jumped with my knapsack!"

How to deal with office politics

Aristotle wrote that "man is by nature a political animal." For evidence, look no further than the workplace. **Glad-handing***. Gossip. Competing interests. Yet few people proudly self-identify as an office politician especially at the entry level. "Young people are often idealistic and see politics as **pathological***," says Richard Shell, professor of legal studies, business ethics, and management at the Wharton School of Business. "They want to be **conscientious*** objectors to office politics, but doing so will limit their effectiveness and leave them **marginalized***." Neutrality is not an option: Ignore office politics, and you put your career in peril. Here is what the experts have to say about **unleashing*** your inner political animal.

1. Politics? What Politics?

"Young workers think, 'I'll **keep** my head down, **my nose to the grindstone***, and be **impervious*** to everything around me,'" says Wayne Hochwarter, professor of management at Florida State University and expert on organizational behavior. "But your actual job function in the office is only one component of work. You need to be aware of an entire social environment, or you'll end up cut off from reality." Develop your **peripheral*** vision and accept that politics is neither good nor bad. No organization has infinite resources, so inevitably people must **jockey*** for time, money, power, promotions, and recognition. In a word: politics.

2. Press the Flesh

Think you're going to thrive by **hunkering*** down in your cube with your headphones on? Think again. Presidential hopefuls practice retail politics—informal campaigning spent shaking hands, chatting at diners, and making personal connections—and so should you. "**Nudge*** yourself to get out, socialize, and network," says Rick Brandon, coauthor of Survival of the Savvy: High-Integrity Political Tactics for Career and Company Success. "Build your visibility." Whether it's a cocktail party or a beer-pong tournament, go. If there's a group of colleagues traveling to hear a speaker across town, join them. Get other people invested in your career—both inside and outside your office. "Think of your contacts and political alliances as a bank account," says Marilyn Puder-York, author of The Office Survival Guide. "Make contributions to it regularly."

3. Cultivate Key Relationships

You know your boss and your immediate colleagues. But how well do you know your boss's assistant? The IT guy? People in finance? The **HR*** department? "Look beyond titles," says Marie McIntyre, author of Secrets to Winning at Office Politics. "For example, many mistakenly assume that people in HR have no power. Well, you'd be surprised at how many problems they solve, how many decisions they influence—even on the level of promotions and layoffs." Bonus: People in departments such as HR and IT sit on a lot of insider knowledge. When an HR person says, "Don't tell anyone, but ..." listen up. Get to know people in finance: They manage long-term budgets and know where the company is headed.

Developing relationships outside your division will help you avoid potential conflicts on projects too. "If you know people on the manufacturing end, in marketing, in sales, you'll be able to anticipate their points of view, their needs, and their agendas," says McIntyre. If you understand these competing interests, you'll be able to navigate the wider political landscape. Just be careful not to confuse work friends for real friends.

4. Good Office Gossip

Sure, office gossip has a negative connotation. But it's not always a bad thing. "Gossip is information," says Asher. "If a colleague you trust warns you before a business trip, 'Hey, that guy always hits on women when he travels,' that might be necessary information for you." Just consider the source. Likewise, you can use gossip for good: If a superior compliments one of your colleagues, tell the colleague. She'll remember your kindness. Gossip can be a valuable currency—especially if you have a reputation for being perceptive, trustworthy, and **discreet***.

When you come across a **nugget*** of information that's genuinely useful to a political ally—a colleague, a networking contact, even a superior—use it to build your alliance: "Normally, I don't share this kind of stuff, but I thought it might help you." That said, keep a couple of rules in mind. First, don't initiate negative gossip or pass it along. Second, be wary of relationships built on too much gossip. "Remember," says Puder-York. "That person who's gossiping with you will probably gossip about you too."

5. Rise Above Conflict

When disagreements arise, try to identify the work-related issue at the source of conflict. If you can't find one, let it go. Head games? **Needling***? Disengage. "I had a younger client who was working with an older colleague who didn't have a college degree," says McIntyre. "The older guy was always Googling obscure information and quizzing the younger guy, trying to trap him. The younger guy was going to go to his boss about this." Bad idea: Generally, do not use your boss as a playground referee to mediate disputes. An exception: If you know someone is going to trash you to your boss, get to your boss first.

The trick is not to return the trash talk, says Brandon. Instead, be the strategic-thinking grown-up, and you can make your **nemesis*** look like an ass. Go to your supervisor and say: "You might be hearing from Tom. We had a disagreement and neither of us was at our best. But if we need to sit down and talk about this, I'm happy to do so."

6. Guard Against Idea Theft

Yes, colleagues may steal your work—and the credit—so get things time-stamped. That means taking your ideas in their available form and running them by your boss or another person with power before they're due, before the big meeting, before anyone has an opportunity to pull a **heist***. Just be careful: It might just be the custom and culture in your company for the head of a team or supervisor to take all the credit for group accomplishments. Try to sidestep the chain of command and you could **burn a few bridges***.

7. Influence, not Power

Power comes from control over resources, hiring, and firing. Early in your career, you may not have much power. But you can build influence by being knowledgeable, competent, trustworthy, and dependable. That sounds obvious, but you need to think about these qualities strategically: not just as virtues in themselves, but as tools to career advancement. Your short-term goal is to make yourself someone whose opinion is valuable. Your long-term goal is to become indispensable. "That means anticipating and knowing what your superiors and colleagues need," says Shell. "It might be your special technical knowledge. It might be your willingness to work on weekends. It might be project-specific. But you'll know when people say, 'We can't start the meeting until Jones gets here.' You want to be Jones."

8. Phrases that Pay

When you receive criticism, you can gently push back by asking specific questions. If you're told you need to be more of a team player or do a better job on your weekly reports, be diplomatic: "Thanks for telling me what I need to work on. Can you be specific about how I can improve?" When you need to give criticism, do it in a tactful way that's unlikely to trigger personal conflict. Phrases that pay: "I'd be doing you a real disservice if I didn't bring this up." "I am concerned about ________ and let me tell you why." "I understand what you are saying and how you see the issue. Let me give you my thoughts."

9. Please the People Who Matter Most

It's not enough to get good results: You need to satisfy the people who matter. That may require hard choices, but you have to make them. "When there's a conflict between the two, choose pleasing your boss over pleasing your colleagues and subordinates, or you will never advance," says Asher. Two prime directives: First, never go over your boss's head without explicit permission. Second, never start a war with your boss. You will lose. Still, keep your first loyalty in the back of your mind: It's not to your boss, your colleagues, or your company. "Your first loyalty has to be to yourself—your brand, your long-term job continuance," says Hochwarter of Florida State. "That includes your profile outside the company where you work in case you need to move on."

10. Don't Complain

You may be low on the political power chain, but you don't have to be a **doormat***. The key is to turn complaints into questions. For example, if people are offloading their work onto you, find the substantive business issue in your complaint, then frame it as a request to get the backup you need. "Prioritizing your work is different from complaining about being overworked," says McIntyre. Don't whine. That's a sure way to enrage your boss. Do go to her and say, "I can help them handle this other work, but could we sit down and I could show you a list of tasks and we could prioritize them?" When others approach you with extra work, say, "I'm glad to help—let me check with my supervisor about that."

11. **Toot Your Horn***

People need to know what you're doing. "I always hear this complaint: 'People just don't know my contributions,'" says McIntyre. "I always ask, 'Why don't they?'" Here's the point: You cannot rely on your accomplishments to speak for themselves. It's up to you to show people your contributions. But when it comes to self-promotion, think storytelling, not advertisement. "Weave your accomplishments into brief narratives that communicate passion, energy, and delight," says Peggy Klaus, the author of Brag!: The Art of Tooting Your Horn Without Blowing It.

If your boss's boss asks how things are going, don't just **chirp***, "Fine." Use the opportunity to mark a specific triumph: "I've been trying to get this difficult customer on the phone for the last two days and I finally did it. He's really **on board*** with us now and I'm thrilled."

1 Key Vocabulary

glad-handing ***n.*** being very friendly to people you have not met before(may be insincere)

pathological ***adj.*** relating to or caused by disease

conscientious ***adj.*** in accordance with conscience or sense of right and wrong; working hard and careful to do things well

marginalized ***adj.*** treated as if not important

unleash ***v.*** to release; to free from control or restraint

keep one's nose to the grindstone ***idiom.*** to work hard and steadily

impervious ***adj.*** not able to be influenced by

peripheral ***adj.*** not relating to the most important part of something; external

jockey ***v.*** to compete for an advantage or a position

hunker ***v.*** to take shelter or settle in

nudge ***v.*** to push gently or slowly

HR ***n.*** Human Resources

discreet ***adj.*** careful to avoid embarrassment, especially by keeping something secret

nugget ***n.*** a small piece

needling ***n.*** provoking or teasing with constant criticism

nemesis ***n.*** a source of harm; an opponent

heist ***n.*** a robbery

burn a few/one's bridges ***idiom.*** to commit oneself to a particular course of action with no possibility of turning back

doormat ***n.*** a person who is physically weak and accepts being treated badly and does not complain

toot one's horn ***idiom.*** to boast about oneself

chirp ***v.*** to make a short, high-pitched sound

on board ***idiom.*** involved in a project or organization, or working for a company

2 For each word in Group A, find the corresponding synonym in Group B and antonym in Group C.

Group A	Synonym	Antonym
a. peril(n.)		
b. socialize		
c. ally(n.)		
d. obscure		
e. trustworthy		
f. enrage		
g. triumph(n.)		

Group B. Synonym	Group C. Antonym
ambiguous	disloyal
accomplishment	opponent

provoke	security
hazard	disaster
mingle	isolate
colleague	apparent
dependable	soothe

3 Match the statement in column A with a related approach to deal with office politics in column B.

	A		B
1	If you know people on the manufacturing end, in marketing, in sales, you'll be able to anticipate their points of view, their needs, and their agendas.	1	Rise Above Conflict
2	You cannot rely on your accomplishments to speak for themselves. It's up to you to show people your contributions.	2	Cultivate Key Relationships
3	Generally, do not use your boss as a playground referee to mediate disputes.	3	Influence, not Power
4	Your short-term goal is to make yourself someone whose opinion is valuable. Your long-term goal is to become indispensable.	4	Press the Flesh
5	If there's a group of colleagues traveling to hear a speaker across town, join them. Get other people invested in your career—both inside and outside your office.	5	Toot Your Horn

HUMOR

A young executive is working late one evening. As he comes out of his office about 8 PM, he sees the Big Boss standing by the shredder in the hallway, a piece of paper in his hand. "Do you know how to work this thing?" the older man asks. "My secretary's gone home and I don't know how to run it." "Yes, sir," says the young executive, who turns on the machine, takes the paper from the other man, and feeds it in. "Now," says his boss, "I just need the one copy."

4 Which of the following is NOT recommended in the passage?

a. Develop your peripheral vision and accept that office politics is neither good nor bad.
b. If a superior compliments one of your colleagues, don't tell the colleague. Keep it as a secret.
c. Build your influence by being knowledgeable, competent, trustworthy, and dependable. Think about these qualities as virtues in themselves, not as tools to career advancement.
d. If people are offloading their work onto you, find the substantive business issue in your complaint, then frame it as a request to get the backup you need.

2 What would you do in the following situations that can happen at any office? Write your solution in about a paragraph.

a. What would you say to your boss if he's crazy about an idea, but you think it is so bad?

____

____

____

____

____

b. How would you tell your co-worker about his/her bad breath or body odor?

____

____

____

____

____

10 powerful fashion tatements made by women in politics

Though we find it unfair that women in politics still have their looks and clothing focused on after they make a speech, we have decided to embrace this and also only focus on what women are wearing despite their political **credentials***. Some of these women use this detailed scrutiny of their ensembles and accessories to their advantage. They power dress. They send a message with their clothing. Who can forget when former Secretary of State Madeleine Albright wore a large American flag pin when she was photographed with North Korean leader Kim Jong Il. It was her way of silently combating North Korean propaganda. That is a fashion statement if there ever was one. Daily Beast's Rebecca Dana wrote, "It isn't easy for path-breaking female public figure—or first female anythings—to balance a feminine aesthetic with the need to act tough in a room full of men." But these women figured out how to do it or at least how to make a statement with their fashion.

Hillary Clinton's pantsuits

Where would we be without Hillary Clinton and her pantsuits? Why **fixate*** on this woman's amazing career and credentials when we can make fun of her hair and uniform of pantsuits. Poor Hillary has been picked on for her fashion sense, or lack there of, for years and she has gotten to the point where she is loudly proclaiming that she doesn't care. "If I want to wear my glasses, I'm wearing my glasses. If I want to pull my hair back, I'm pulling my hair back. At some point it's just not something that deserves a whole lot of time and attention," she told CNN. "If others want to worry about it, I'll let them do the worrying for a change."

Margaret Thatcher's pearls

If the internet had been around when Margaret Thatcher served as Prime Minister of England, you can bet there would have been some **Tumblrs*** and **Memes*** dedicated to those pearls she always wore. The conservative

Thatcher actually cared very much about her appearance. She worked with style consultants tirelessly to make sure she was presenting the perfect image of power. She kept a hairdresser on staff and put aside time each day to select an outfit including a tasteful pair of high heels. And though they had to work on Margaret toning down some of her more feminine attributes like her voice and her love for hats, Margaret and her team also realized that power of the feminine touch. This may have been why Thatcher insisted on wearing those pearls. She still has quite an effect on professional women even though she hasn't been in office since 1990. According to a new survey, women are **emulating*** some of Margaret Thatcher's most well-known traits to try to get ahead in the workplace. Just as the former Prime Minister was given **elocution*** lessons to help her "too-feminine" voice and sported power suits to make her seem more authoritative, women today are adopting throatier voices, wearing longer **hemlines*** and displaying less cleavage.

Madeleine Albright's pins

You know your accessory has power when a whole collection is inspired by it. In 2009 the Museum of Art and Design in NY held an exhibition called, "Read My Pins: The Madeleine Albright Collection." It featured some 200 brooches the former secretary of state had collected over the years. Robin Givhan of The Washington Post wrote of Albright's pins: "Albright intentionally shopped flea markets and costume jewelry boutiques to build her collection so that it would not be fancy or **rarefied***. The brooches are valuable only because of their **provenance***. They were chosen and worn by the first female secretary of state, one who understood that fashion, rather than being a burden, could be another tool in her diplomatic arsenal. And it was one that men did not have."

Imelda Marcos's shoes

This woman had so many pairs of shoes that now people use her name as a benchmark if they have a lot of something. For example, I could be the

Imelda Marcos of cheap scarves bought on the street. The former beauty queen had several positions in the government when her husband became President of the Philippines in 1965. Marcos left behind 2,700 pairs of shoes when she was forced to leave the Malacanang Palace in exile. "They went into my closets looking for **skeletons***, but thank God, all they found were shoes, beautiful shoes," Marcos said. In 2001 she opened a shoe museum. The exhibits include shoes made by Ferragamo, Givenchy, and Chanel, all size eight-and-a-half.

Jackie Kennedy's everything

Name one thing Jackie Kennedy wore during not only her time as First lady, but for the rest of her life, that wasn't amazingly fashionable. From the pearls to the hats to the beautiful Givenchy dresses to that tragic pink Chanel suit she wore the day JFK was killed. Everything Jackie wore was a statement. Designers such as Givenchy, Chanel, Lanvin, and Jason Wu create designs with the style of a modern-day Jackie Kennedy.

Sarah Palin's everything

I thought I could narrow it down to just her glasses but with Sarah it was really the whole package. It was Palin's appearance as much as her politics that **catapulted*** her into the spotlight. Her look was so **intriguing*** because it was a blend of "I want to be taken seriously" with the glasses and outdated hairdo and then with sexy secretary attire. But what it really meant was how her look was contrasting next to Hillary's. The New York Times said, "Anything Hillary can do, our gal from Anchorage can do better, including avoiding that **hideous*** orange trouser suit and replacing it with something much more becoming to the complexion. This has to be one of Palin's wisest decisions so far: breaking up a **rootin'-tootin' color*** with black trousers, and ensuring that the light reflects on her biggest asset, the beauty-queen face. Any allusions to soft and peachy skin are entirely intentional."

Michelle Obama's dresses

She has been called The First Lady of Fashion. Like everything else she does, a lot of thought goes into her ensembles. They are high class but attainable as evident in her **affinity*** for J. Crew. After Obama wore J. Crew on "The Tonight Show" and a White House/Black Market dress on "The View," the pieces sold out the next day. She also stands out among female political figures because she embraces colors and feminity. When Obama wore a modified cocktail dress by Narciso Rodriguez on Election Night, she stood out dramatically next to Jill Biden, Sarah Palin and Cindy McCain in traditional suits. She has a **Jackie O*** like quality but with a modern and more relatable twist.

Nancy Pelosi's purple ensembles

Nancy Pelosi, Speaker of the House, has a **go*** to color and it is purple. The Daily Beast noted that she wore her favorite lavender suit and pearls to President Obama's first State of the Union address. She wore eggplant for a March 2 press conference to discuss the state of health-care reform negotiations outside her congressional office in Washington. Her look is grownup and feminine, not mannish in the least. Here is a mother of five, who obviously has spent plenty of time taking temperatures and feeding spoonfuls of cough medicine to sick kids—certainly more time than she's spent at **Barneys***, agonizing over what to wear. It is a challenge but you can dress feminine and still be taking seriously.

Christine Lagarde's scarves

Christine Lagarde is French and she wants everyone to know. The Managing Director of the IMF made it on to Vanity Fair's Best Dressed List due in large part to her perfect blend of high French **couture*** with business attire. Her use of scarves in her outfits is absolutely strategic as it can brighten up her whole outfit and set her apart from all the men in dark suits in the world

of international finance. Forbes' Raquel Laneri wrote, "Like the **canniest*** political and business people, she uses style to assert her individuality and dominance amid a set of suits. Who else, for example, would have worn a pink scarf for her first press conference as managing director of the IMF? Take her wide array of scarves. Lagarde often **jazzes up*** her suits with scarves the way Michael Douglas wears red suspenders in *Wall Street*: to set herself apart and to assert her power. And she wears her scarves with such French **insouciance***—casually knotted or thrown around her neck. So effortless. It's exact opposite of what most women in powerful positions do."

Ann Romney's red dress

Did you know a dress could have political **subtext***? According to the media, Ann Romney's choice to wear a beautiful red Oscar de la Renta dress for her speech at the Republic National Convention was full of subtext. We're not sure if that was the intention but the dress definitely made a statement. Her look said I am ready to be First Lady and screamed I love America. In the Daily Beast, Pulitzer-Prize winning fashion columnist Robin Givhan described Romney's look at the RNC as "a classic vision of a first lady." "The dress gave her a polish and glow that the speech did not. So even if her words didn't reveal much, the packaging was pitch perfect," Givhan wrote. "The cinched-waist silhouette gave off a '50s homemaker **vibe*** that surely cast Romney in a more relatable light to more than a few women in the audience, despite its four-figure price tag," Stylite explained.

1 Key Vocabulary

credentials ***n.*** personal achievements, or experiences that make someone suitable for something

fixate ***v.*** to direct and focus on

Tumblr ***n.*** a social networking website founded by David Karp

Meme ***n.*** an idea, behavior or style that spreads from person to person within a culture

emulate ***v.*** to copy something achieved by someone else

elocution ***n.*** the art of public speaking in which gesture, vocal production, and delivery are emphasized

hemline ***n.*** the length of a skirt or dress

rarefy ***v.*** to make or become rarer

provenance ***n.*** the place of origin; the history of the ownership of an object

skeleton ***n.*** 1. something reduced to its minimal form
2. a scandal that is kept secret
3. idiom: *skeleton in the closet*
an embarrassing secret about your past that you do not want anyone to know

catapult ***v.*** to throw with great force

intriguing ***adj.*** very interesting because of being strange or mysterious

hideous ***adj.*** extremely ugly

rootin'-tootin' ***adj.*** exciting; cheerful and lively

affinity ***n.*** a natural liking towards a person or thing

Jackie O ***n.*** Jacqueline Lee Bouvier Kennedy Onassis(July 28, 1929-May 19, 19, 1994). She was the wife of the 35th President of the United States, John F. Kennedy, and served as First Lady from 1961 until his assassination in 1963. She was later married to Greek shipping tycoon Aristotle Onassis from 1968 until his death in 1975.

go ***n.*** energy; an attempt to do something

Barneys ***n.*** an American chain of luxury department stores

couture ***n.*** expensive and fashionable high quality clothes of original design

canny ***adj.*** careful and clever in dealing with others

jazz up ***v.*** to make something more interesting or lively

insouciance ***n.*** lack of care or concern

subtext ***n.*** a hidden meaning

vibe ***n.*** (short for vibration) a feeling you get from a person or place

2 What does each underlined expression refer to?

a. *Margaret Thatcher*: She worked with style consultants tirelessly to make sure she was presenting the perfect image of power. She kept a hairdresser on staff and put aside time each day to select an outfit including a tasteful pair of high heels. And **they** had to work on Margaret toning down some of her more feminine attributes.	
b. *Madeleine Albright*: The brooches were chosen and worn by the first female secretary of state, one who understood that fashion, rather than being a burden, could be another tool in her diplomatic arsenal. And it was **one** that men did not have.	
c. *Imelda Marcos*: Marcos left behind 2,700 pairs of shoes when she was forced to leave the Malacanang Palace in exile. "**They** went into my closets looking for skeletons, but thank God, all they found were shoes, beautiful shoes," Marcos said.	
d. *Sarah Palin*: "Anything Hillary can do, our gal from Anchorage can do better, including avoiding that hideous orange trouser suit and replacing it with something much more becoming to the complexion. **This** has to be one of Palin's wisest decisions so far."	
e. *Ann Romney*: Her choice to wear a beautiful red Oscar de la Renta dress for her speech at the Republic National Convention was full of subtext. We're not sure if **that** was the intention but the dress definitely made a statement.	

3 Find the words and phrases in the passage that match these definitions.

a. beautiful quality ____________ (1st para.)
b. to be worthy of ____________ (para. about Hillary Clinton)
c. a standard by which others may be measured or judged
____________ (para. about Imelda Marcos)
d. an unexpected change ____________ (para. about Michelle Obama)
e. a blackish purple ____________ (para. about Nancy Pelosi)
f. to make someone/something different or special
____________ (para. about Christine Lagarde)
g. a dark image seen against a light background
____________ (para. about Ann Romney)

4 Converse with your partner about the politicians' fashion. You are a newspaper reporter. And your partner is a political analyst.

Example:

Reporter: a. Why do you think Ms. Pelosi always wears purple?
b. Why do you think Ms. Imelda collected that many shoes?

Political analyst:
a. As far as I know the color purple means elegance and power. I think that's why she wears purple to show both of them.
b. ____

5 Here is an example of political license plates. Make your own plate for one of the politicians in the passage.

(Source: http://www.smartblonde.net)

Chapter 7

Lifestyle

Vacations let us loosen time's grip

I have taken time off. Literally. The watch that straps my workaday wrist to its demands sits on the kitchen shelf. I have **shed*** its manufactured time, its minute hand, hour hand, just the way I shed my city wardrobe, makeup, pantyhose, skirt. Gradually I have even begun to lose track of time. First the minute and then the hour, finally the day. My watch and I have wound down.

I **reckon*** that my real vacation starts the moment I forget whether it is Thursday or Friday. And the moment I realize that it doesn't make any difference. At last, I tell myself, I have slipped out of one time frame and sunk into another. I have left a world divided by nothing more than numbers, 60 minutes, 24 hours, seven days a week. I have entered a world of seasons: blueberry, raspberry, blackberry season; lobsters that shed old shells and then harden new ones.

My daily life here is connected more to the tide than to the time. At low tide I can harvest the mussels that lie under great heaps of seaweed clinging to rocks by their **umbilical*** beards. At high tide the mackerel may swim in hot pursuit into the **cove***. The cove is not a store with hours set by its owner.

Like most people in the Western world, I have grown up in the artificial environment of modern society. It's a place dominated by external time-keepers, calendars, schedules, clocks. Our lives are subdivided into fiscal years, academic years, weekdays, weekends, deadlines. We are taught that there is a time to get up, a time to go to work, a time to eat. We set the clock by a single standard.

Time orders our lives and, inevitably, orders us around. We are so removed from natural rhythms that we rarely confront how "unnatural" this is. How unnatural to strap time on. But we didn't always live with this artificial timing. In "Time Wars," Jeremy Rifkin explains just how recently people have been **alienated*** from their natural rhythms to those of the schedule, the clock and now the computer with its nanosecond culture. The schedule—that control on our lives—was the invention of the Benedictine monks whose early passion for organizing and filling every minute of the day grew from St. Benedict's warning that "idleness is the enemy of the soul." His followers reintroduced the Roman hour and invented the mechanical clock.

Not until the 15th Century did clocks, those icons of **temporal*** time, begin to rival churches in the city squares. Not until the 17th Century did clocks have a minute hand. "Medieval time," writes Rifkin, "was still **sporadic***, leisurely, unpredictable and above all tied to experiences rather than abstract numbers." It was the merchants and factory owners who eventually, and with great difficulty, trained workers—those who had previously lived in accord with the seasons—to become as regular as clockwork. Today, writes Rifkin, "the high achievers see time as an obstacle to overcome, an enemy to defeat. They equate faster and faster learning with victory over time; to win is to beat the clock."

Is it any wonder that many of us choose vacations that stretch uninterrupted from sunrise to sunset, choose to re-enter the natural cycle, days of idleness, that friend of the soul? Is it any wonder that we seek, for just a while, not to think of time as a commodity to be spent, saved, wasted, used, but to live from tide to tide?

My own escape is hardly complete. A creature of habit more than habitat, I have yet to spend a day without once looking at a clock or asking the hour. My vacation itself is **circumscribed***. I have only a certain amount of time allotted to timelessness. It will end at a pre-determined moment. I will go home according to the boat schedule. But on this day the ghostly white impression left by the watch on my arm has finally browned. I can barely see its imprint on my life.

1 Key Vocabulary

shed ***v.*** (shed-shed) 1. to get rid of something that is not wanted or is no longer necessary; *The firm is going to shed 1000 jobs.*
2. to let something fall off as part of a natural process

reckon ***v.*** 1. to calculate 2. to consider that something is true

umbilical ***adj.*** relating to a long tube that connects an unborn baby to its mother, through which it receives oxygen and food

umbilical beards of mussels

cove ***n.*** a small area of a see, river, or lake that is partly surrounded by land

alienated ***adj.*** feeling that you do not belong in a particular society, place, or group

temporal ***adj.*** 1. relating to or limited by time: *Music is a temporal art.*
2. relating to ordinary life rather than religious matters: *He wanted much more than mere temporal power and wealth.*

sporadic ***adj.*** occurring at irregular intervals; having no pattern or order in time

circumscribe ***v.*** 1. to draw a line around something
2. to limit something such as power, rights, or opportunities

2 Add a suffix to each word and complete the sentences with the new words.

-ly	-ment	-en	-er	-ion	-ness

own____	gradual____	idle____	impress____
hard____	environ____	rare____	invent____

a. My first __________ was that I finally found what I had been searching for.
b. The popular phrase "killing time" refers to __________ and can be defined as spending time doing nothing in particular.
c. I very __________ wear a raincoat because I spend most of my time in the office.
d. The __________ of the store was sweeping the floor when I walked in.

e. Put the meat in the freezer awhile to ________ it up before you try to slice it thin.
f. Where did Louis Pasteur come up with the idea for his ________?
g. They believe nuclear power causes a serious threat to the ________.
h. In the election campaign office, the mood ________ changed from victory to defeat.

3 Read each statement and identify if it is a fact or an opinion.

a. Our lives are subdivided into fiscal years, academic years, weekdays, weekends, deadlines.
b. At low tide I can harvest the mussels that lie under great heaps of seaweed clinging to rocks by their umbilical beards.
c. Not until the 15th Century did clocks, those icons of temporal time, begin to rival churches in the city squares.
d. A creature of habit more than habitat, I have yet to spend a day without once looking at a clock or asking the hour.

4 Famous Quotes about Time

Q When your friends begin to flatter you on how young you look, it's a sure sign you're getting old. — Mark Twain

Q He that is not handsome at 20, nor strong at 30, nor rich at 40, nor wise at 50, will never be handsome, strong, rich or wise. — George Herbert

Q Time stays long enough for those who use it. — Leonardo da Vinci

Q Don't watch the clock; do what it does. Keep going. — Sam Levenson

Q Young men wish; love, money and health. One day, they'll say; health, money and love. — Paul Géraldy

Q The young feel tired at the end of an action, the old at the beginning. — T. S. Eliot

Q No man knows he is young while he is young. — Gilbert Keith Chesterton

Q Even a stopped clock is right twice a day. — Marie von Ebner-Eschenbach

Q I never really did years of movie-after-movie-after-movie but when you've got three toddlers in the house you're performing all day long, anyway, with puppet shows and stories—I act around the clock. — Julia Roberts

Q Time invested in improving ourselves cuts down on time wasted in disapproving of others. — Unknown Source

Q Youth is happy because it has the ability to see beauty. Anyone who keeps the ability to see beauty never grows old. — Franz Kafka

Champagne corks should never take off, for safety or taste

The popping of champagne corks is an evocative sound, symbolic of **gaiety*** and celebration. What many champagne drinkers don't realize, however, is that expelling a cork with such force that it rockets through the air like a missile can be dangerous. It is also counter-productive.

A special technique is required for uncorking champagne and other sparkling wines to assure that all of the bubbles are retained, no wine is spilled and no damage is done to life, limb or property. Champagne is special precisely because of its bubbles, so an effort should be made to preserve them. The cork should be removed carefully and gently to avoid the explosion that means much of the gas has been lost. After the lead or paper foil around the cork has been stripped away, the wire holding the cork in place should be removed while one hand is firmly on top of the cork, to assure that it will not be expelled **prematurely***. Then the cork should be gripped tightly and the bottle turned with the other hand. Turning the bottle, rather than the cork, enables you to grip the cork continuously and prevent it from flying out.

When the cork begins to rise out of the bottle, it should be held tightly and rocked from side to side to enable excess carbon dioxide to escape around the sides. A gentle hissing lets you know this is happening.

When the hissing ceases, the pressure will have **abated*** and the cork can be removed easily. During this procedure, the bottle obviously should be aimed away from one's face or nearby lamps, windows, paintings or anything else fragile, just in case the grip on the cork is lost. Some corks are ready for launch at the least movement and can fly without warning. They are capable of seriously damaging an eye, breaking a window or denting a ceiling.

Occasionally a cork will prove stubborn and need to be removed with a pair of pliers or one of the so-called **champagne wrenches***. The worst that can happen is for the top of the cork to break off, leaving the rest in the neck of the bottle. Then a corkscrew must be used to extract the remnant, which can be extremely dangerous lest the cork suddenly be expelled with the corkscrew attached. If the top of the cork does break away, use great care and grip the handle of the corkscrew tightly with one hand while holding your other hand around the screw itself as it penetrates. This should act as a safeguard against losing control if the cork suddenly pops out under pressure.

1 Key Vocabulary

gaiety ***n.*** a state of being merry, bright, or lively

prematurely ***adv.*** occurring, growing, or existing before the customary, correct, or assigned time; uncommonly or unexpectedly early

abate ***v.*** 1. to reduce in amount, degree, or intensity
2. to become less active or intense

champagne wrench

2 Collocation

effort noun

1) *V. make*: The workers should make all reasonable efforts to improve productivity. / *continue, intensify, concentrate, direct*: We must concentrate our efforts on tackling crime in the inner cities. / *abandon, block, frustrate*: It is premature to abandon efforts to understand and promote positive phenomena

among people with various life-threatening illnesses. / *reward, support*: Their efforts were supported by donations from friends, family and co-workers. / *pay off, succeed*: All our efforts paid off when we received the Best Designed and Innovative Furniture Award.

2) ***ADJ.*** *considerable, massive, determined, every, sustained*: Considerable effort has been made to increase student interest and competency in the fields of science and technology. We must make every effort to avoid the evils of war. / *collaborative, combined, joint*: Conference attendees seek joint effort on rare earth minerals. / *futile, vain, wasted*: Artists have written books, painted paintings and made great sculptures in a futile effort to recapture their lost youth. / *final, last*: Should I make one last effort to her?

3) ***Prep.*** *with/without*: This can be done quickly and with very little effort. / *through*: Through personal efforts, he has set up a 24-hour ambulance service that has helped save the lives of scores of passengers. / *in*: Changes were made in operating methods in an effort to increase profitability.

3 Grammar Focus

Then a corkscrew must be used to extract the remnant, which can be extremely dangerous *lest* the cork suddenly *be* expelled with the corkscrew attached.

Lest is used in very formal contexts to indicate that an action is done in order to prevent a possible negative outcome. It is followed by *should* or, more formally, by a subjunctive form(the base form of the verb).

a. He was scared lest he should fail the exam.
b. Susan turned the TV down lest she miss the phone ringing.
c. He fled the country lest he be captured and imprisoned.

Cross-word puzzle

Across

1. easily broken or damaged
4. to take hold of it with your hand
5. to send something into the air
6. a power tool with a fixed or adjustable jaw
8. to make less active or intense
10. to force something out from a container

Down

1. a thin flexible sheet of metal
2. having the power to bring to mind
3. a metal object with a spiral line around it
4. a state of being merry
7. to make a sound like long ‘s’
9. something left over

A sample sale at Hermès defies the Wall Street malaise*

The line stretching along 18th Street between Avenue of the Americas and Seventh Avenue at lunchtime this week did not look like a crowd of women accustomed to waiting. A few wore dark pinstripes or carried Wall Street Journals; many wore heels and oversize sunglasses. About a third seemed to be wearing some variation of the **ubiquitous*** cloverleaf charm necklace (the one made by Van Cleef & Arpels; on the Upper East Side, it's the modern-day version of pearls), and some significant percentage were casually **toting*** a Birkin bag, or at least a pretty faithful **knockoff*** of that classic Hermès tote, which starts at a cool $8,000 (before tax—and isn't discounted anywhere).

Women dressed like that **hop out*** of driver-navigated **Escalades*** to wait in only one kind of line: the kind that leads to a killer sample sale. This particular line was for Hermès, best known for its luxury leather goods, scarves and ties, whose sample sale started, by invitation only, on Tuesday, and then was opened to the public until Sunday. Wall Street may have turned into one big **fire sale***, but that is apparently not enough to dampen the **perennial*** feverish enthusiasm for a sample sale, even one where bargains are defined as a $900 pair of boots or a $280 leather-bound hunting horn the size of a comb. It's not that the women in line were unaware of the scent of financial disaster **hovering*** in the air. To the contrary, more than one was waiting there to get away from it.

"I just needed a break," said a banker who waited, on crutches no less, for well over an hour on Tuesday. "You know it's not going to be a good year for anyone. But some things are recession-proof, and this sale is one of them. Even if I don't find anything, I still spend a thousand. It's like Costco." That shopper would not give her name or say where she worked, since she probably should have been at the office, under the circumstances. "Let's just say my bank's still around," she **demurred***. "That narrows it down to about four." "Stop bragging," said someone ahead of her in line. The women said they were shopping for relief; they were also shopping because in their world, that kind of shopping represented a form of economizing.

"Even if the economy's down, a sale is all the more reason to buy something nice," said a young woman in a dark, sharply tailored suit. Like the banker ahead of her, she declined to give her name, on the grounds that she was supposed to be at the office—in her case, helping to prepare Securities and Exchange Commission filings to comply with new hedge-fund regulations. She folded her Wall Street Journal under one arm. "Buy something nice, it makes you look good. If you look good, you feel good. If you pay full price and things are unstable at your job, it takes away the enjoyment."

There is always that other option. "Not to buy?" she asked. She shook her head. "That wouldn't work." No one seemed to be considering the possibility that a few months from now she might not have a job to dress up for. Then again, there's no more pressing time to buy a high-prestige morale boost than when you might be dressing for job interviews.

Some were there because scarves, unlike stocks, at least look pretty forever. "I used to buy Sirius stock to keep myself from buying more Hermès scarves," said Jan Goode, who was wearing a coral one and carrying a tote she had made to **showcase*** another one. Ms. Goode, who is in her 50s, considers herself a serious collector of Hermès scarves, stopping just short of considering herself someone with a serious problem. "Now my Hermès holdings are much more valuable than my Sirius stock," she said. "Sirius is at 90 cents a share. I should have been buying scarves all along."

After 9/11, there were many public arguments that seem vaguely absurd in retrospect—that irony was over, or that getting out and shopping to **bolster*** the economy could be an act of patriotism. Oddly, that particular rationale—shop to keep America strong—did not come up in the Hermès line on Tuesday afternoon, although almost every other one did. "It makes you feel a little better—like maybe there's some normalcy in the world," said a tall woman. "Driving in, I was feeling guilty all the while," said the woman behind her, who lives on Long Island. Her husband's construction business, like so much else, has been dead. "What right do we have to be here?" she asked. "We don't!" said the woman in front of her. "I'll only buy if it's something I really need," **resolved*** the woman from Long Island, as if she might enter the sale to find, alongside $2,000 jackets, $300 change purses and $200 toddler robes, essentials like light bulbs, toilet paper or toothpaste.

When the prices of vintage Hermès scarves go down on eBay—then we'll really know we're in trouble.

1 Key Vocabulary

malaise ***n.*** a general sense of depression or unease
ubiquitous ***adj.*** seeming to be everywhere at the same time
tote ***v.*** to carry
n. a bag capable of containing a large quantity
knockoff ***n.*** an unauthorized imitation
hop out ***v.*** to get out of quickly
Escalades ***n.*** a full-size luxury sport utility vehicle sold by the General Motors luxury brand, Cadillac
fire sale ***n.*** a sale of goods supposedly damaged by fire; an occasion, usually very brief, for buying at specially reduced prices
perennial ***adj.*** lasting throughout the year or through many years
hover ***v.*** to be suspended in the air
demur ***v.*** to show reluctance
showcase ***v.*** to display
bolster ***v.*** to support; to boost
resolve ***v.*** to reach a decision/conclusion (after a discussion or deliberation)

2 Complete the sentence with the correct form of the words in the box.

tote(*v.*), dampen(*v.*), crutch(*n.*), tailor(*v.*), vague(*adj.*), resolve(*v.*)

a. You can make your injury worse and even create new injuries with __________ that are used improperly.
b. The services are attractively priced and are __________ to suit individual needs.
c. In order to __________ a conflict, you'll need to look at the conflict from your opponent's point of view.
d. If I even __________ understood your question, I would certainly try to answer it.
e. The stylish bags are the perfect accessories to __________ all your goods.
f. Economists agree that short-term increases in oil prices have __________ the economy and hurt consumer confidence.

3 What does each of the following underlined expressions refer to?

a. Paragraph 2: Wall Street may have turned into one big fire sale, but **that** is apparently not enough to dampen the perennial feverish enthusiasm for a sample sale.	
b. Paragraph 3: Even if I don't find anything, I still spend a thousand. **It**'s like Costco.	
c. Paragraph 5: There is always that other option. "Not to buy?" she asked. She shook her head. "**That** wouldn't work."	
d. Paragraph 6: Jan Goode, who was wearing a coral one and carrying a tote she had made to showcase **another one.**	
e. Paragraph 7: Oddly, that particular rationale—shop to keep America strong—did not come up in the Hermès line on Tuesday afternoon, although almost **every other one** did.	

4 Abbreviations and acronyms commonly used in fashion industry

ACC = accessories
CWD = casual working dress
ES = extra small; extra short
GL = genuine leather; German look
HUGS = hats, underwear, gloves, and socks
LBD = little black dress
MD = marked down
OSFA = one size fits all
RTW = ready to wear
SXL = super extra large
UDJ = unwashed denim jacket
WD = wedding dress
BTSC = back to school clothing
DL = double layered
FPS = four piece suit
HH = high heels
KISS = keep it simple and sassy
LS = long sleeve
MWZ = men's with zipper
PKT = pocket
SI = slightly imperfect
TUX = tuxedo
VEL = velcro
YL = young ladies

5 Write some features of a bag you want to buy for yourself or for your girl friend.

e.g., water- and stain-proof
capable to stand up by itself

1.

2.

3.

4.

5.

6 Find the synonyms for the following words and circle them in the puzzle.

significant	bargain	brag	comply	absurd	bolster

I	R	I	D	I	C	U	L	O	U	S	R
M	S	Q	R	N	C	D	B	W	I	K	X
P	V	B	X	J	W	O	F	B	K	U	S
O	F	O	L	L	O	W	G	M	T	C	J
R	M	J	T	I	S	S	H	R	H	A	K
T	Z	D	V	B	C	T	O	U	E	W	M
A	D	V	L	J	P	P	Z	F	S	R	K
N	W	T	R	H	P	B	O	A	S	T	N
T	C	X	T	U	M	G	M	D	O	O	X
M	S	D	S	S	E	J	O	P	S	Q	B
D	W	M	M	L	I	X	Z	Z	C	B	A
L	A	G	R	E	E	M	E	N	T	O	U

Chapter 8

People

Designing a simple society

Imagine you have suddenly been transported back in time 100,000 years. You find yourself amidst a group of cave dwellers. Because they have been immensely impressed by your advanced knowledge, they ask you to help them redesign their whole society. So you sit down and help them prepare a list of all the vital tasks that must be performed adequately in order to sustain the group. Your aim is to divide these tasks up so that they are performed efficiently, thus providing the group with the highest possible standard of living.

As you attempt to match people to jobs, you make a profound discovery, one the cave dwellers have always known. Age and sex greatly determine to which jobs people should be assigned. It just isn't sensible to send children out to hunt wild animals or to fight enemy tribes. Nor is it feasible for women to perform tasks that separate them from their infants, since nursing is the only way infants can be fed. In addition, women are smaller than men and are often pregnant, which limits their physical mobility. You soon see that women in this society should perform those tasks that can be done close to the cave so that they can care for their infants and supervise children too young to care for themselves. Tasks far from the cave that require the greatest strength must be performed by the men. This division of labor is universal in primitive societies.

This is the only sensible way to divide the tasks. Unfortunately, it has many consequences. Those people most familiar with the issues involved will dominate decision making pertaining to those issues. The two most urgent areas of decision making, because they are the most difficult ones for the group to control, are hunting and fighting. Should we move in search of a better supply of game? Can we survive against the tribe on the other side of the forest? Thus, in addition to being able to dominate women by strength alone, men in simple societies gain dominance because of the particular tasks they perform. Although women's tasks are vital to the survival of the group, men's tasks involve immediate threats to survival. For example, if the women are lax in caring for their infants, the group may slowly die out. If the men are lax about defense, the group may be wiped out in a few hours.

Having designed your simple society, you soon discover something else. Different tasks call for different skills, especially for different kinds of personalities and different styles of interaction. In a world where keeping enough infants and children alive is a constant struggle, a group will have a better chance of survival if the women are tender and loving, but survival chances diminish if the men are like that. You soon realize that your society needs aggressive, somewhat cold-hearted fathers and gentle, somewhat warm-hearted mothers. But how can this be accomplished? The answer has always been differential socialization.

You must raise boys and girls differently so that they will develop different kinds of personalities and regard their differences as desirable and natural. That is, socialization will be most effective when both mothers and fathers treat sons and daughters in consistently different ways, encouraging the boys to be tough and brave and the girls to be gentle and maternal. As a result, males and females will be different.

Thus we see how sex roles came to be firmly established. Moreover, it is not surprising that these patterns of differential socialization tended to mislead people into assuming that the very different personality traits of men and women were inborn. Today, of course, many of these beliefs about the sexes have been rejected. But the fact of markedly different gender socialization mostly remains. While differential socialization begins in infancy, it continues throughout the life cycle. It is useful, therefore, to examine sex-role socialization at various stages in life.

1 Vocabulary Expansion

Complete the following table with the appropriate words. The word-formation may not be the same for all of them.

verb	*noun*	*adjective*	*adverb*
impress	impression		
	sense	sensible	
survive		surviving survivable	
	desire		desirably

2 Find the word from the passage which matches each definition.

a. qualities and traits, as of character or behavior, that are peculiar to a specific individual: ___________

b. to control, govern, or rule by superior authority or power: ___________

c. belonging to an early stage in the development of humans: ___________

d. wild animals, birds, and fish that people hunt, usually for food: ___________

3 Identify if the following expressions in the passage are related to males, females, or both.

nursing, dominance, cold-hearted, tender and loving, cave-dwellers, tough and brave, gentle and maternal, differential socialization
perform those tasks that can be done close to the cave, tasks far from the cave that require the greatest strength, those people most familiar with the issues involved, two most urgent areas of decision making

Males	
Females	
Both	

HUMOR

Things Mom Would Never Say

"How on earth can you see the TV sitting so far back?"
"Yeah, I used to skip school a lot, too."
"Just leave all the lights on ... it makes the house look more cheery."
"Let me smell that shirt—Yeah, it's good for another week."
"Go ahead and keep that stray dog, honey. I'll be glad to feed and walk him every day."
"Well, if Timmy's mom says it's OK, that's good enough for me."
"The curfew is just a general time to shoot for. It's not like I'm running a prison around here."
"I don't have a tissue with me ... just use your sleeve."
"Don't bother wearing a jacket—the wind-chill is bound to improve."

Controlling crimes in the society

If a society is to continue to function smoothly, then the members of that society need to behave in orderly ways: they need to follow certain norms and obey certain rules. How does it happen that most people in a society agree to obey the rules? According to sociologists, there are two kinds of controls that influence the way an individual behaves. These are referred to as *internal controls* and *external controls*.

Imagine you are in a music store and you see a CD that you want. The price is $20. You have only $5 with you, but the thought of stealing the CD does not occur to you. Why not? The answer is internal controls. Internal controls are those you impose on yourself based on your values, beliefs, and fears. One of the values you hold is that stealing is wrong and that honesty is right and good. To continue to feel good about yourself, you don't steal. So the first aspect of internal control is how you feel about yourself. The second aspect of internal control is the possible **disapproval*** of friends and family who might become aware of your stealing. You do not want to have to talk with your parents or husband or wife or children or friends about why you stole a CD. The third factor operating to discourage you from stealing is the fear of being arrested. Many shops display signs such as "This store **prosecutes*** **shoplifters*** to the full extent of the law" and employ store detectives to identify shoplifters. Finally, social forces such as whether you are employed full-time may influence whether you steal or not. You may be afraid of social consequences, such as losing your job or losing the trust of your work colleagues.

For some individuals internal controls will not be enough to deter them from breaking the law. Most societies also impose external controls or punishments of some kind to discourage people from committing crimes.

There are three main kinds of external controls: public embarrassment; the payment of money, or fines; and **imprisonment***. If a police officer stopped you for speeding, you would probably be embarrassed as other passing motorists stared at you. If you were going fast enough, you would also be asked to pay a fine as well as court costs. If you were driving while drunk, you would be taken to jail, fined, and have your driver's license taken away from you.

There are a number of factors that influence the effectiveness of these external controls in stopping people from committing crimes. Their effectiveness depends, for example, on how certain it is that the crime will be punished. If there is little likelihood of being caught, the external controls may be weak or ineffective. It also depends on how severe the punishment is. The threat of being sent to prison is more likely to prevent people from breaking the law than the threat of paying a small fine. For some crimes, external controls do not seem to be very effective. For example, a person who commits a "crime of passion" is in a state of uncontrollable rage or feels overwhelming pressure and may not give any consideration at all to the consequences of his or her actions.

1 Key Vocabulary

disapproval ***n.*** a feeling of hating something or what someone is doing
prosecute ***v.*** to carry out a legal action against someone
shoplift ***v.*** to steal something from a store
imprisonment ***n.*** putting someone in prison as a punishment

2 Complete each sentence with an appropriate word.

disapproval	deter	internal	fine(*n.*)	stare(*v.*)	consequence

a. Don't let frustration ____________ you from your goal.
b. A wine retailer faces a heavy ____________ for not recycling its waste.
c. Most people know lung cancer can be an unhealthy ____________ of cigarette smoking.
d. There's nothing wrong with staying out of the ____________ affairs of foreign countries.
e. He will give a look of ____________ to stupid, insensitive, or just plain disgusting comments.
f. I ____________ out the window wishing I could fly away from here.

3 Write a creative warning message to prevent shoplifting.

4 Grammar Focus

Some verbs are typically followed by an object and a prepositional phrase with -ing form.

discourage deter stop prevent	something someone	from	-ing

Here are some examples from the passage.

a. The third factor operating to **discourage** you **from** steal**ing** is the fear of being arrested.
b. For some individuals, internal controls will not be enough to **deter** them **from** break**ing** the law.
c. There are a number of factors that influence the effectiveness of these external controls in **stopping** people **from** committ**ing** crimes.
d. The threat of being sent to prison is more likely to **prevent** people **from** break**ing** the law than the threat of paying a small fine.

5 Famous Quotes about Crime

Q I believe that the high rates of property crime are part of the price you pay for freedom. — James Wilson

Q The most difficult crime to track is the one which is purposeless. — Arthur Conan Doyle

Q Anybody who doesn't know that politics is crime has got a few screws loose. — James Ellroy

Q Growing old is like being increasingly penalized for a crime you haven't committed. — Teilhard Chardin

Q The idea that the sole aim of punishment is to prevent crime is obviously grounded upon the theory that crime can be prevented, which is almost as dubious as the notion that poverty can be prevented. — H.L. Mencken

Darkness at noon

Blind from birth, I have never had the opportunity to see myself and have been completely dependent on the image I create in the eye of the observer. To **date*** it has not been **narcissistic***.

There are those who assume that since I can't see, I obviously also cannot hear. Very often people will converse with me at the top of their lungs, **enunciating*** each word very carefully. Conversely, people will also often whisper, assuming that since my eyes don't work, my ears don't either.

For example, when I go to the airport and ask the ticket agent for assistance to the plane, he or she will invariably pick up the phone, call a ground hostess and whisper: "Hi, Jane, we've got a 76 here." I have concluded that the word "blind" is not used for one of two reasons: Either they fear that if the dread word is spoken, the ticket agent's **retina*** will immediately detach, or they are reluctant to inform me of my condition of which I may not have been previously aware.

On the other hand, others know that of course I can hear, but believe that I can't talk. Often, therefore, when my wife and I go out to dinner, a waiter or waitress will ask Kit if "*he* would like a drink" to which I respond that "indeed *he* will."

The toughest misconception of all is the view that because I can't see, I can't work. I was turned down by over forty law firms because of my blindness, even though my qualifications included a *cum laude* degree from Harvard College and a good ranking in my Harvard Law School class.

1 Key Vocabulary

date ***n.*** the present moment; now

narcissistic ***adj.*** having too much admiration for oneself; having an excessive idea of one's importance

enunciate ***v.*** to pronounce words clearly so that they can be easily understood

retina ***n.*** a light-sensitive tissue lining the inner surface of the eye, which sends light signals to your brain, where they are changed into images

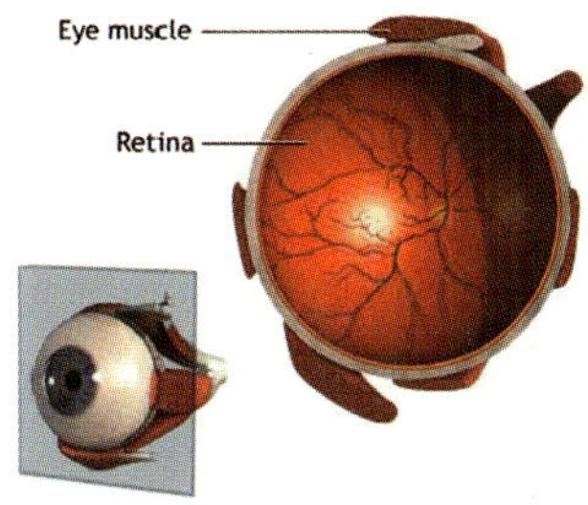

2 Read the following text and choose the most appropriate words for the blanks.

Guide Dogs

People who cannot see at all, or whose sight is very poor, can find some things hard to do, without some help. One of their biggest _____1_____ is getting around. Imagine crossing a busy road when you can't see the traffic. Imagine walking past bus stops, parked cars, and bicycles that you cannot see. A guide dog _____2_____ its blind or partially-sighted owner to get around safely and independently. It guides its owner in a straight line, unless told _____3_____, avoiding obstacles—including those at the owner's head height. It will stop at curbstones and steps and find doors, crossings and places that are visited regularly. It will guide its owner across the road, but it is the owner who decides where and when to cross safely. The guide dog and its owner are a _____4_____, with the owner giving commands and encouragement and telling the dog which way to go. The dog is not a miracle worker, but for some people it can offer a safe and effective way of getting about independently.

1. a. performances b. challenges c. threats
2. a. enables b. allows c. directs
3. a. so b. otherwise c. twice
4. a. model b. route c. partnership

3 Famous Quotes about Being Blind

Q There's none so blind as those who won't see. — English proverb

Q Painting is a blind man's profession. He paints not what he sees, but what he feels, what he tells himself about what he has seen. — Pablo Picasso

Q Kindness is the language which the deaf can hear and the blind can see. — Mark Twain

Q If your eyes are blinded with your worries, you cannot see the beauty of the sunset. — Jiddu Krishnamurti

Q Love, like a chicken salad or restaurant hash, must be taken with blind faith or it loses its flavor. — Helen Rowland

Q Bitterness imprisons life; love releases it. Bitterness paralyzes life; love empowers it. Bitterness sours life; love sweetens it. Bitterness sickens life; love heals it. Bitterness blinds life; love anoints its eyes. — Harry Emerson Fosdick

Q The sun gives us light, but the moon provides inspiration. If you look at the sun without shielding your eyes, you'll go blind. If you look at the moon without covering your eyes, you'll become a poet. — Serge Bouchard

Q With most people, doubt about one thing is simply blind belief in another. — G. C. Lichtenberg

Q Absolute faith can blind you to the consequences of the actions you allow. It can tell you it's okay to drop bombs on another country, or that it's okay to hate a group of people such as homosexuals. — Andrew Denton

Q Parents are traffic signs that are always in our blind spots. — Jeremy P. Johnson

Q If thou art a master, be sometimes blind if a servant, sometimes deaf. — Thomas Fuller

The wallet

When Elaine arrived at work the first thing she noticed was that Troy had left his wallet on the small shelf next to a half-finished cup of Coke. Troy left his food regularly, as if she were his maid, but he left his wallet less often—about once a month. The first time it happened was just her second night on the job, and she thought maybe he was testing her, or, worse, that he had created some excuse to come back and see her. He had, in fact, returned half an hour later and deliberately rubbed his body up against hers as he retrieved his wallet instead of just standing at the door and asking her to hand it to him. They had made awkward small talk in the **cramped*** booth before he finally raised his wallet in a salute, said good-bye and good luck and rubbed past her again.

Now, as she settled onto the stool for her shift, she could smell his lingering presence. She picked up the cup of Coke and placed it in the garbage can at her feet, careful to keep it upright. The cup had sweated out a puddle in the summer heat and she shook her head **despairingly***. She lined up her files of quarters and dimes on the shelf in order to have something to do. Two booths down, Jose waved at her and gave her two thumbs up, a gesture he thought was cute. He was another **lecherous*** type, always spending his breaks standing at her door looking her up and down and blowing smoke into her booth. She waved at him so he'd turn around.

In front of her now the highway was black. Every few minutes headlights would appear in the distance like slow trains but most of the time the drivers would pick the automatic lanes. Then three or four cars might come in a row and she'd be grateful to move into a rhythm—reach, grab, turn, gather, turn, reach, good night. It was annoying when people didn't bring their cars close enough, but at least it allowed her to stretch more. By midnight she had made change for twenty-six people. Several weeks ago she had started to keep track out of boredom. Her midnight record was seventy-two, her fewest, twelve.

At about three o'clock a car came toward her too fast, weaving like a firefly, before picking her booth. The brakes screeched, the muffler roared: it was a little yellow Chevettte, an eighties car **pocked*** with rust. Elaine leaned forward with her hand ready, but the driver, a young woman, made no move to pay her toll. She looked straight ahead, her face hidden by strings of brown hair, both hands locked tight to the wheel. Beside her in the front seat was a small **beat-up*** suitcase overflowing with clothes.

Elaine said, "Good morning," and the woman said, "I need money." Elaine hesitated, "You mean you don't have the toll?" "No, I mean I need money." She turned now and Elaine saw her **bleary*** eyes and **splotched*** face. There was an ugly gash below one eye and the skin around it had swollen up and turned purple. There seemed to be an older scar on her nose, and dried blood in the corner of her mouth. Her stare was bitter and bold and it made Elaine look away. She was about to raise the bar and tell her to go on ahead when she saw movement in the backseat. Looking closer, she saw there were two children, one about five, the other barely two, neither in car seats or seat belts. Their eyes were wide and afraid and Elaine realized it was this that had drawn her attention to them in the dark. The little one held on to a gray stuffed animal, the older one was sucking her thumb.

Jose was watching her; he raised his palms and **scowled***. She had been trained to signal in a certain way if she was being held up, and Jose seemed to be waiting for this gesture. Instead, she gave him a thumbs up and **surreptitiously*** reached for Troy's wallet. She opened the wallet to find ninety-two dollars inside. She pulled these bills out, **wadded*** them in her fist and reached out to the woman, who took the money, gripped the wheel harder and sped away. The older girl's face, framed by the back window, receded into the darkness, her eyes like glowing stones.

1 Key Vocabulary

cramped ***adj.*** uncomfortably small or restricted
despairingly ***adv.*** with a feeling that a situation is so bad that nothing you can do will change it
lecherous ***adj.*** characterized by excessive interest in sexual activity
pocked ***adj.*** having marks on your skin that go inward
beat-up ***adj.*** damaged or worn because of neglect or heavy use
bleary ***adj.*** looking dull or tired as if you have not had enough sleep or have drunk too much alcohol
splotched ***adj.*** marked with irregularly shaped spots
scowl ***v.*** to show an angry or hostile expression on one's face
surreptitiously ***adv.*** in a secret way
wad ***v.*** to roll into a bundle

2 Complete each sentence with an appropriate word.

rub	salute	roar	barely	recede

a. The sound of a freight train is the __________ of wind as it moves through trees and buildings. It may indicate an approaching tornado.

b. Just as I started to think that I was never going to get well, the illness began to __________.

c. I wanted so much to give him a __________ to show him my deep respect.

d. __________ down the door and wash off the dust before applying the varnish.

e. I can __________ remember the sound of your voice.

HUMOR

You're driving too slowly!

There was this car that was driving very slowly down the highway. A police officer pulls it over. "What have I done wrong, officer?" the driver asks. "You are going 26mph on a major highway. There is a law against that," the officer says to the driver. "You must go at least 50mph." "But when I turned on the highway, the sign said 26!" the driver replies. "HA HA HA!" The officer laughs out loud. "That is because this is Interstate 26! The 26 isn't the speed limit!"

The driver leans back in her car seat and the cop sees another woman sitting beside her. She looked as pale as a ghost. "What happened to her?" the officer asks. "I don't know, but she has been that way ever since we got off of Interstate 160."

3 Grammar Focus

She opened the wallet ***to find*** ninety-two dollars inside.

'To' before the base form of a verb is used when indicating what situations comes after a particular action.

a. She grew up to start a new life on her own in London.

b. He awoke to discover that he had overslept.

c. He lived to be twice as old as his youngest son did.

4 **Let's suppose the woman who got the money from Elaine wrote a letter to her a few months after the incident. What would the woman say?**

Victims vs. Oppressors

When I walked in the front door Sunday afternoon, Sara was pacing back and forth like a caged lion. Her face was flushed. She was trembling from the **waning*** effects of the adrenalin that had been pumping through her body minutes before. I knew my first words should be more sensitive than, “Hi, honey, I’m home. What’s for dinner?” Sara had just returned from the supermarket at Sixth Street and Washington Avenue in South Philadelphia, where there had been another incident. There have been several of these incidents during the twelve years she had shopped there, but this was the worst. It started, as usual, in the checkout line. She was in the express line when a group of maybe five teenage boys walked up with some items and a couple of the teenagers pushed in front of her. Sara is one of those people who reacts to rudeness by speaking up rather than **simmering*** in silence and frustration. She told them that she was there first and they could get in line behind her. Big mistake.

The boys, in the 14-16 age range, began to make insulting remarks. “We can get in front of you if we want to,” they muttered. Two of them pushed in front of her in line, and the other three were behind her. The remarks continued. Sara asked them to **lay off***, and they began mimicking her language: “Lay off, she wants us to lay off.” Sara looked around. The cashier could easily see and hear what was going on, as could other customers. But no one wanted to do anything. This was her problem. She was invisible in a crowded place. Welcome to the New York subway.

They were waiting for her when she got outside. She figured she could leave the packages and get the car, in which case the food might be stolen, or she could walk to the car with her arms loaded and take that chance. She walked. They followed. They were punks, neighborhood toughs picking on a lone woman. What did they want? Maybe if she hadn’t said anything

... . When Sara reached the car, they surrounded it. Then they sat on the hood. She asked them to get off, and they laughed at her. She put the packages inside the car. She asked them to get off the car again, and their **taunts*** grew bolder. Then it happened.

Sara had been describing this to me in a trembling voice, and when she reached this part, she demonstrated what happened. "I slammed the door of the car, and I walked up to the one who had started it all and I went like this," she said, grabbing me hard by the **lapels***, pushing me against the wall at the same time she pulled my face close to her face, which was twisted in rage, "If you don't get off my car, you stupid ..., you're dead!" she said.

Now to fully appreciate this, you'd have to know Sara. First of all, she is not a big woman, about 5-foot-6, and her face leans more to "sweet" than "tough." But I had no trouble believing she was capable of this display of **imprudent*** temper(I call her an iron fist inside a velvet glove), and I also believed that this would have a **riveting*** effect on a 5-foot-10 teenager, considering that during the demonstration she almost lifted her 6-foot-3 husband off his feet.

The other thing you have to appreciate is that we don't use words like Sara used on these toughs. But here was Sara, surrounded by a gang, **lunging*** at the **ringleader***, making **Frank Sinatra threats**[+] and giving these kids a lecture in urban realities using urban "get out of my face" language. After she pushed off from the stunned teenager, she got in the car, started the engine, gunned the motor, put it in gear, and the kids scattered as she pulled away.

I looked at her in alarm and unbelievable pride. "That was a stupid thing to do," I said, obligatorily. For the first time, she began to realize what she had done. She had been so caught up in the moment that she hadn't considered the extent of her action. Unarmed, unescorted women do not grab and threaten five menacing teenage boys. "Who do you think you are, Sara Goetz[++]?" I said. Then I laughed. We both laughed.

Sure it was a dumb thing to do, sure I could be writing a column with an entirely different ending right now. But I'm not, am I? If you choose to live in the city, you take your chances. To get all the good things that are to be had by city living, you run the risk of encountering the bad. There are many things Sara could have done to have avoided this situation—the first being nothing at all. But sometimes you get tired of being timid and you lash out at those who would take your city away from you. And sometimes that pure rush of righteous anger can stun those who would bully you, who would paralyze you through intimidation, who would make you feel small and powerless.

Are you wondering whether these boys were white or black? If so, ask yourself this: Does it matter? All race does is **cloud*** the issue, and the issue here is victim versus oppressor. It's so rare when the victim turns the tables, and when that happens, we cheer. We see that, and we think to ourselves, let that be a lesson to the predators of our cities.

As for you, Sara, don't you ever, ever, ever do something like that again.

[+]: A full description of the expression is given at Exercise 2 below.

[++]: The reference here is to William Goetz, who shot several youths who threatened him on a New York subway.

1 Key Vocabulary

waning ***adj.*** (wane *v.*) decreasing gradually in size, amount, intensity, or degree

simmer ***v.*** to cook slowly at or just below boiling point

lay off ***v.*** 1. to end the employment of a worker, especially temporarily, because there is not enough work for them
2. to stop doing something

taunt ***n.*** an unkind or insulting remark, especially about one's weaknesses or failures

lapel ***n.*** the part of a garment, such as a coat or jacket, which is an extension of the collar and folds back against the breast.

imprudent ***adj.*** unwise, by failing to consider the likely results of your actions

riveting ***adj.*** extremely fascinating

lunge ***v.*** to move suddenly and with a lot of force in order to catch, hit, or avoid something or someone

ringleader ***n.*** a person who leads others in any kind of unlawful activity

cloud ***v.*** 1. to cover with or as if with clouds: *A sudden mist clouded the hills.*
2. to make less visible or clear: *The big tower clouds our view of the mountain.*
3. to become gloomy or depressed: *In that moment, his face clouded, his eyes dimmed and the pain he carried was noticeable.*

2 What do you mean by "Frank Sinatra threats"?

When the novel "The Godfather" was published, Frank Sinatra (1915-1998) was furious at the author of the book, Mario Puzo (1920-1999), because he believed that he served the author as an inspiration for the fictional mobster, singer and actor in the book, Johnny Fontane. But Puzo claimed that the character was not based on Sinatra. When Sinatra met Puzo at Chasen's restaurant in Hollywood in 1970, he screamed vulgar terms and threatened to break Mario Puzo's legs.

3 Find the word from the passage which matches each definition.

a. to talk in a low and indistinct tone; to make complaining remarks or noises: ________

b. to shut a door or window with force and loud noise; to throw something against or onto a surface with great force: ________

c. to perform an action at high speed; to move or shift fast into a new position or place: ________

d. an annoyed or impatient feeling that you get when you are prevented from doing what you want: ________

e. a feeling of intense anger; a strong emotion that is oriented toward some real or supposed grievance: ________

f. threatening to cause you harm or put you in danger whether it is on purpose or not: ________

g. one that victimizes or destroys for one's own gain: ________

4 **What do you think of Sara's behavior in the situation? If you were Sara, would you have done the same thing as Sara or would you have avoided the confrontation with the kids? Write a rationale for your choice.**

Chapter 9

Arts

Art and music therapy for Alzheimer's disease

There is no known **magic bullet*** for Alzheimer's disease. There are, however, many ways to treat symptoms and problems associated with the disease. Some Alzheimer's treatments involve medications. Others are non-medical Alzheimer's therapies like art, music, and more. The goal of an Alzheimer's therapy is to help the person maintain a better quality of life.

Alzheimer's therapies that draw on individual interests through structured activities can be beneficial. Which therapies might work best for your loved one with Alzheimer's disease? Start to answer this question by thinking about his or her past hobbies or passions. Talk with the doctor as well, who may have more suggestions and resources for using these therapies effectively for Alzheimer's disease.

Music Therapy for Alzheimer's Disease

Music therapy has many benefits for Alzheimer's disease. It may help by:

- Soothing an **agitated*** person
- Sparking memories
- Engaging the mind even in the disease's later stages
- Improving eating in some cases

Here are some tips for using music therapy to help your loved one:

1. Golden oldies spark memories. Songs from the person's youth often spark the most memories. In the later stages of Alzheimer's disease, you may have to go back to songs learned in childhood. Encourage sing-alongs. Try using a karaoke machine.
2. Toe-tapping beats stimulate activity. **Up-tempo*** dance tunes can help stimulate both mental and physical activity in Alzheimer's patients. Encourage dancing, if possible.
3. Easy listening can be soothing. Soothing music can help ease the anxiety and frustration felt by many people with Alzheimer's disease. For example, lullabies at bedtime can help your loved one get into bed and fall asleep.

A person with Alzheimer's disease may not be able to verbally communicate their likes and dislikes. Rely on other clues such as facial expressions to help you learn which songs are a hit and which aren't. Ask friends or relatives for suggestions about the types of music or particular songs the person used to enjoy.

Art Therapy for Alzheimer's Disease

Painting, drawing, and other forms of art therapy can help people with Alzheimer's disease express themselves. Expression through art can become especially important as a person's ability to communicate through words **deteriorates***.

Here's how to get your loved one engaged in art therapy:
1. Picture the past. Encourage a project that tells a story or evokes a memory. The project can be something that you can talk about together, both while the work is in progress and after it is finished.

2. Free form. Keep instructions to a minimum to avoid confusion and frustration. Then, step out of the way as the work takes shape. If necessary, get things started by painting the first few brush strokes yourself to remind your loved one how it is done. Don't forget that the picture is done when the person says it's done, whether you think so or not.
3. Don't be a critic. If you don't care for the colors chosen, keep it to yourself! Positive feedback and questions that are **conducive*** to interaction are the best contributions you can make.

Other Alzheimer's Disease Therapies

Other therapies can help **enrich*** the life of a person with Alzheimer's disease. Which therapies work best depends on the needs of the individual.

• Massage. This hands-on therapy may help in two ways. It can ease agitation and may improve sleep.

• Pet therapy. People who used to enjoy being with pets may find contact with them enriching or soothing. Match the pet to the person's needs. For example, a person who can walk may enjoy visiting with a dog. A person who is less mobile may enjoy petting a cat.

• Previous hobbies. Pursuing hobbies or interests that used to be familiar can help a person with Alzheimer's feel more stable about their lives. Consider gardening, cooking, or any other activity that the person used to enjoy. Try to work these activities into the person's daily routines.

1 Key Vocabulary

magic bullet *n.* something that solves a difficult problem easily; a remedy that cures a disease with wonderful properties or easily without side effects

agitated *adj.* (agitate v.) troubled emotionally; physically disturbed

up-tempo *adj.* having a fast or lively beat

deteriorate ***v.*** to become worse or lower in quality, character, or value

conducive ***adj.*** 1. tending to assist: *You should try to keep good eating habits conducive to good health.*

2. being partly responsible for: *The new seaport was a conducive factor in the growth of the region.*

enrich ***v.*** to make rich; to improve in quality; to make more rewarding

2 Write the adjective form(e.g., -able, ing, tive, or ate) of each of the following verbs. Then complete the sentence with the correct adjective.

treat ________	encourage ________	maintain ________
stimulate ________	deteriorate ________	engage ________
consider ________	communicate ________	

a. Two pounds a week is a ________ weight loss and limits the yo-yo effect.

b. Aging is defined as the ________ changes during the adult period of life that underlie an increasing vulnerability to challenges.

c. Congressional Budget Office says unemployment benefits have the strongest ________ effect on the economy.

d. The goal of language acquisition is ________ competence.

e. Being ________ to others is not an absolute necessity in life, however, it tends to make social interactions easier.

f. The power of a single glance or an ________ smile must never be underestimated.

g. Blood clots can be deadly, but they are often preventable and ________.

h. The class can help you gain some teaching tips on how to make science ________ to middle school students.

3 Which of the following is NOT true according to the passage?

a. In deciding the best therapy for a person with Alzheimer's disease, it is better to begin by asking what their past interests were.
b. In the early stage of Alzheimer's disease, songs learned in childhood are helpful.
c. Even with Alzheimer's disease, people are able to verbally express their likes and dislikes.
d. In doing art therapy, the instructor should step out of the way while the work of the person with Alzheimer's disease takes shape.
e. A person with Alzheimer's disease who is less mobile may enjoy visiting with a dog.

4 Famous Quotes about Music

Q Music washes away from the soul the dust of everyday life. — Berthold Auerbach

Q Of all the music that reached farthest into heaven, it is the beating of a loving heart. — Henry Ward Beecher

Q Love is like a violin. The music may stop now and then, but the strings remain forever. — June Masters Bacher

Q Opera is when a guy gets stabbed in the back and, instead of bleeding, he sings. — Ed Gardner

Q Music expresses feeling and thought, without language; it was below and before speech, and it is above and beyond all words. — Robert G. Ingersoll

Q Life can't be all bad when for ten dollars you can buy all the Beethoven sonatas and listen to them for ten years. — William F. Buckley

Q A musician must make music, an artist must paint, a poet must write, if he is to be ultimately at peace with himself. — Abraham Maslow

Q Music is a moral law. It gives soul to the universe, wings to the mind, flight to the imagination, and charm and gaiety to life and to everything. — Plato

Broadway's big night is over

Musical comedies have fascinated New York ever since the **inception*** of Broadway, the theaters on and around the Great White Way. But the theater district's **heyday*** in the Roaring Twenties, when it staged nearly 50 new musicals in a season, is a distant memory. Far fewer shows open now. They cost a lot more to stage. Too many are revivals or old hits as producers seek to reduce the risk of backers suffering crippling losses.

As a result, interest centers around the finances of the musical theater rather than the stars and the writer-composer teams. *Variety*, a show-business weekly, used to be the only source of financial information on the incoming, on-going, and out-going musicals. Today the money troubles of shows are reported in the tabloids, and readers of a gossipy weekly column in the *New York Times* can learn, for instance, that a prize-winning Gershwin **pastiche*** *Crazy for You*, took 725 performances to repay its investors their $8.3 million; that *Miss Saigon* got back its $10 million in less than half that time; and that *The Will Rogers Follies* did not **recoup*** its original cost during its long Broadway run.

Such **daunting*** statistics strike fear into the hearts of producers and investors alike. Courageous **impresarios*** still exist, even on a Broadway **strewn*** with lavish theater **marquees*** announcing that shows have closed (or which never arrived) and shuttered glass doors that display ticket refund information. But this season, more money seems to be being invested in revivals or in imports of proven material than in new, original shows.

1 Key Vocabulary

inception ***n.*** the start of an institution or activity

heyday ***n.*** the time when a particular person or thing had great importance and popularity

pastiche ***n.*** a musical composition consisting of a series of songs or other musical pieces from various sources

recoup ***v.*** to get back money that you have invested or lost

daunting ***adj.*** (daunt v.) feeling worried because you think that it will be very difficult or dangerous to do

impresario ***n.*** one who sponsors or produces entertainment

strew ***v.*** (strewed-strewn/strewed) to cover (an area or a surface) with things scattered

marquee ***n.*** 1. a cover over the entrance of a building, for example, a theater

2. a large tent which is used at a fair, garden party, or other outdoor event, usually for eating and drinking in

2 Etymology of the word 'gossip'

The word is from Old English *godsibb*, from *god* and *sibb*, the term for the godparents of one's child or the parents of one's godchild, generally very close friends. In the 16th century, the word assumed the meaning of a person, mostly a woman, one who delights in idle talk. In the early 19th century, the term was extended from the talker to the conversation of such persons. The verb *to gossip*, meaning "to be a gossip", first appears in Shakespeare. The term originates from the bedroom at the time of childbirth. Giving birth used to be a social (ladies only) event, in which a pregnant woman's female relatives and neighbours would gather. As with any social gathering there was chattering and this is where the term gossip came to mean talk of others.

Cross-word puzzle

Across

2. separated in space
4. spending too freely
8. frightened or worried
10. to pay back
11. bringing again into activity

Down

1. to attract you very strongly
3. a regular article in a newspaper
5. the period of greatest success
6. money returned to a payer
7. new and different from anything else
9. to give information about something to a person

Graffiti: Is it vandalism or contemporary art?

People have been painting and writing on walls throughout history. In prehistoric times, people in Africa and Europe used to paint pictures of animals and people in caves. Carved on the buildings at ancient sites in Greece, Italy, Syria and Iraq are many example of graffiti. In the Roman town of Pompeii, archaeologists have found numerous examples of graffiti written in Latin. These include religious, political and romantic messages, and even some magic spells!

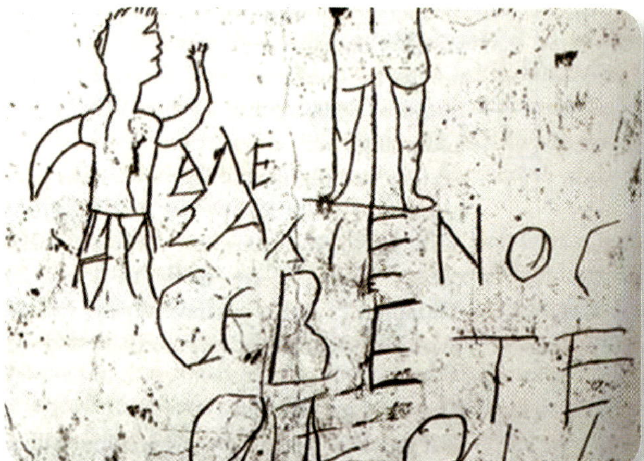

In modern times, graffiti and street art became an international phenomenon. In the 1970s, young people in New York used pens to write their names or "tags" on walls around the city. One of the first "taggers" was Demetrius, a teenager from a Greek family. Demetrius's tag was TAKI 183. TAKI was his nickname and 183 was the number of the street he lived on—183rd Street. At first, he wrote his tag on walls in his neighborhood. Then he started tagging in subway stations on the way to and from school. When the subway train stopped at a station, he would jump off, write his tag on the wall and then jump back on before the doors closed. Other teenagers noticed Demetrius's tag and started to write their own. Soon, New York's walls, buses and subway trains were covered with tags: Barbara 62, Joe 182, etc.

Later on, some teenagers started writing tags with **aerosol*** paints. Their tags were bigger, more colorful and took more time and imagination than the simple, pen-written tags. The trend spread and from the 1970s, aerosol paint graffiti became a common sight on trains, buses and walls in cities around the world. In the 1990s, graffiti continued but there was also an explosion in street art around the world. Some artists wanted to make political points and produced art that tried to make people think about war, inequality and discrimination. Other street artists were more concerned with producing beautiful, attractive work. In South America, many street artists went to work in poor areas adding color, life and beauty to grey, city walls.

Is graffiti art or **vandalism***? This depends on your point of view, but in many countries, writing or painting on public or private property is considered vandalism. Many street artists have been stopped by the police and some have had to pay fines. Many city councils complain about the high cost of cleaning graffiti off buildings, buses and trains. In some countries, councils have tried to encourage artists not to paint randomly on walls by allowing them to work in designated areas. In Taiwan, there are "graffiti zones" where artists are free to paint and write on walls. In Sao Paulo in Brazil, the city council has even allowed some graffiti artists to paint on the city's subway trains. And what does the art world think of graffiti and street art? Recently, there has been a growing recognition of its value as an art form. There have been major exhibitions of street art in galleries in Paris, London and Los Angeles. American artist Elura Emerald organized a street art exhibition at a New York Gallery in 2008. She defended street artists, saying "artists who paint on the street are merely expressing themselves, not hurting anyone. They should be appreciated and celebrated."

Most street artists are anonymous, but others have become globally famous. Here are two stars of the street art world. Blek le rat started out painting rats on the walls of his home city, Paris. He now tries to make people think about different social issues and problems. He paints pictures of homeless people in big cities to encourage residents to think about the problem of homelessness. Faith 47 is from Cape Town in South Africa. She paints big, colourful pictures of people and animals. Her work is found on **pavements***, in empty factories and on abandoned cars. She likes the fact that most street art is temporary and will soon be removed by weather or cleaners from the city council. For her, this reflects how life is full of change with its cycle of endings and new beginnings.

It is impossible to know how street art will develop in the future but certain trends are emerging. While most street artists are young people who paint in their city or neighborhood, more and more street artists are traveling and working around the globe. Other artists are using the internet to talk to each other and share photos of their work. Also, the art world is giving more recognition to street art as a **legitimate*** art form. Although we don't know what will happen to street art in the future, we can be sure that it is here to stay!

Winner of the All Ironlak Graffiti Competition 2010 (Source: http://www.invurt.com)

1 Key Vocabulary

aerosol ***n.*** a liquid substance, such as paint, an insecticide, or a hair spray, packaged under pressure for use or application as a fine spray

vandalism ***n.*** the act of deliberately damaging or destroying things, especially public property

pavement ***n.*** a hard smooth surface, especially of a public area or a road from one place to another

legitimate ***adj.*** in accordance with law

2 Add a prefix or suffix to each word. Then complete the sentences using the words.

_____national(*adj.*)	_____courage(*v.*)	attract_____(*adj.*)
homeless_____(*n.*)	_____equality(*n.*)	random_____(*adv.*)
_____historic(*adj.*)	exhibit_____(*n.*)	

a. A career in fashion is becoming increasingly __________ to young people.

b. The new pop art ___________ opens at the Birmingham Museum and Art Gallery on 17 November.

c. __________ between rich and poor is rising at most nations.

d. Nuclear weapons have returned to center stage in __________ affairs.

e. No experience necessary, only a desire to serve, an ability to work with other people, and a sensitivity to problems of __________ and poverty.

f. The __________ ages date back to the Early Stone Age, which lasted from the first appearance of man to the end of the last Ice Age around 10,000 B.C.

g. __________ your child to reach a compromise between what he wants and what you want.

h. There is no real evidence that a ____________ selected sample of public school students will perform better in a private school than in a public school.

3 Grammar Focus

Carved on the buildings at ancient sites in Greece, Italy, Syria and Iraq are many example of graffiti.
<< Many examples of graffiti are carved on the buildings at ancient sites in Greece, Italy, Syria and Iraq.

A lexical verb(the main verb of the sentence) with an accompanying complement may sometimes be placed at the beginning of a sentence for the purpose of focusing on some other element of the verb phrase. The part which is moved to the beginning may be followed by subject-verb inversion, especially in formal styles.

a. Hidden in the heart of modern Turkey lie the scattered ruins of a long-forgotten civilization.
b. Run the marathon was what she did.
c. Attached to this email is my investment proposal.
d. Sitting at the chair asleep was he with a cake on his lap.

4 Answer the following questions and share the answers with your partner.

a. What do the examples of graffiti found in Pompeii exhibit?

b. What did the two-word tags usually refer to?

c. What is your own opinion about graffiti? Is it vandalism or art?

d. How does the famous French street artist try to make people think about different social issues and problems?

e. How is graffiti being treated by the art world?

5 Funny Graffiti

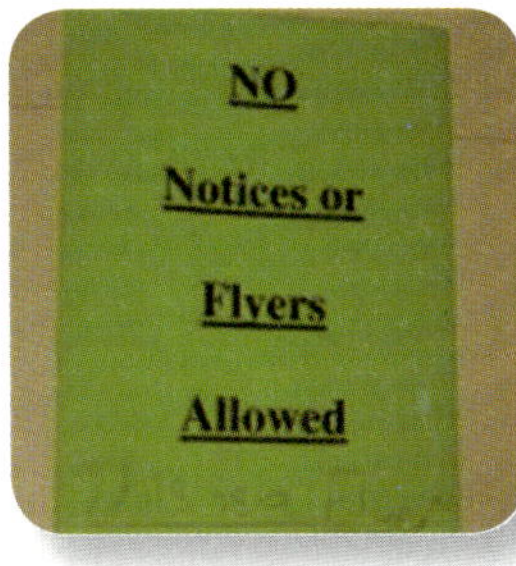

6 Write your own graffiti on the wall.

Stunt school

Think you've had a rough day? Try this. First, you get thrown out of a car onto the expressway. Next, you fall out of a tree. Then you tumble down the stairs headfirst. To top it off, you get set on fire ... and it isn't even noon yet!

For graduates of a Toronto stunt school, this is all in a morning's work. Since opening its doors, Stunt Production Canada has trained hundreds of would-be stunt performers. They come from all **walks of life***—lawyers, firefighters, retail workers, hockey players, factory workers, and almost anyone else you can think of. The glory, excitement, and big pay of movie stunt work can be a powerful **draw***. But most people who take the Stunt Productions courses—$1,000 for the introductory course, plus another $720 for the advanced—don't intend to make a full-time career in the movies.

A qualified stunt performer working on a unionized Canadian film set earns a minimum of $342 a day, and top stunt performers can earn $150,000 a year or more. Big names in the business can earn $500,000 as year doing stunts and consultation work for major films. But most stunt school students will never earn more than the cost for their tuition—they're not looking for a movie career, just something that's different from their everyday lives. And they get it—drops, fights, crashes, burns, drags behind cars—all are part of the school's 16-week introductory course. Those who want more can take the 12-week advanced course.

Almost every student who has enrolled in the school since it opened has been male, and few are over 30. In the stunt business, 40 is considered ancient. So why do people want to be stunt performers? "I do it because it's fun!" says Craig Samuel, who's used his stunt school diploma to get a few movie parts. "Stunt men tend to be people searching for the edge. The trick is whether you go over it or not. I don't usually tell people I'm a stunt man," he says. "They always say, 'Oh, you're a **daredevil***!' But you're not a daredevil. The key to stunt work is being careful so you don't get hurt. I don't want to die."

Despite the precautions the pros take, there is danger. "Of course there's danger," says school owner Parr. "Stunt men get killed sometimes. It happens." Dar Robinson, the famous stunt man who jumped twice from the **CN Tower*** for movies, was killed riding a motorcycle during a routine, low-risk film sequence.

"It was pretty ironic," Parr says. "When you consider all the dangerous things he'd done."

"If you're not prepared to get banged around a little bit, you shouldn't be in it," says Samuel. "Some mornings you can't get your head off the pillow."

1 Key Vocabulary

walk of life ***n.*** an occupation, profession, or social class

draw ***n.*** 1. one that attracts interest, customers, or spectators
2. a contest ending without either side winning

daredevil ***n.*** one who enjoys doing physically dangerous things

CN Tower a communications and observation tower in Downtown Toronto, Canada. Its name "CN" refers to Canadian National, the railway company that built the tower.

2 Complete the sentence with the correct form of the words in the box.

tumble draw drag edge precaution sequence consider

a. He was such a popular __________ that his talk had to be switched to a larger venue.

b. Many of the world's ports were closed and planes grounded as a __________ against terrorism.

c. Gold prices __________ in trading today, suffering their biggest one-day loss.

d. Reckless spending is being a __________ on the economy.

e. The film's opening __________ is of a very unpleasant murder.

f. All things __________, you're utilizing your limited time to the best of your ability.

g. The brisk walk gave some __________ to my appetite.

3 Commonly used terms in filmmaking

ad lib	shortened from *ad libitum*, a Latin phrase meaning at your pleasure, used to mean spontaneous or improvised.
antagonist	a character, group of characters, or institution that stands in opposition against which the protagonist(s) must contend. In other words, an antagonist is a person or a group of people who oppose the main character(s).

cameo	a brief appearance or voice part of a known person in a film. Many of them are non-speaking ones, and are commonly either appearances in a work in which they hold some special significance (such as actors from an original movie appearing in its remake), or renowned people making uncredited appearances.
director's cut	a rough cut that is supposed to represent the director's own approved edit. It is preceded by the rough editor's cut and followed by the final cut meant for the public film release.
diffusion gel	a transparent, tinted colored sheet of plastic used as a filter for a movie light to soften subjects and generate a dreamy haze. It may have a clear center area to create a vignette of diffused area around the clear center subject.
long shot	a camera shot from a great distance, usually showing the characters as very small in comparison to their surroundings. An extreme long shot can be taken from as much as a quarter of a mile away, and is generally used as a scene-setting, establishing shot.
mise en scène	design aspects of a film production, which essentially means "visual theme" or "telling a story"—both in visually artful ways through storyboarding, cinematography and stage design, and in poetically artful ways through direction.
persona	a social role or a character played by an actor. It is derived from Latin, where it originally referred to a theatrical mask.
Q rating	a measurement of the familiarity and appeal of a celebrity used in the United States. The higher the Q Score, the more highly regarded the person is among the group that is familiar with him/her.
stunt double	a stunt performer that takes the place of an actor when the scene calls for a dangerous or sophisticated action.

Chapter 10

Learning

Why do language learners make errors?

There are two main reasons why second language learners of English make errors. The first reason is influence from the learner's first language (L1) on the second language. This is called interference or transfer. Learners may use sound patterns, **lexis*** or grammatical structures from their own language in English. The second reason why learners make errors is because they are unconsciously working out and organizing language, but this process is not yet complete. This kind of error is called a developmental error. Learners of whatever mother tongue make these kinds of errors, which are often similar to those made by a young first language speaker as part of their normal language development. For example, very young first language speakers of English often make mistakes with verb forms, saying things such as 'I goed' instead of 'I went'. Errors such as this one, in which learners wrongly apply a rule for one item of the language to another item, are known as overgeneralization. Once children develop, these errors disappear, and as a second language learner's language ability increases, these kinds of errors also **pass off***.

Errors are part of learners' interlanguage, i.e., the learners' own version of the second language which they speak as they learn. Learners unconsciously process, i.e., analyze and reorganize their interlanguage, so it is not fixed. It develops and progresses as they learn more. Experts think that interlanguage is an essential and unavoidable stage in language learning. In other words, interlanguage and errors are necessary to language learning.

When children learn their mother tongue, they seem to speak their own form of it for a while, to make progress on some language items, then to go backwards, and to make mistakes for a time before these mistakes finally disappear, usually without obvious correction.

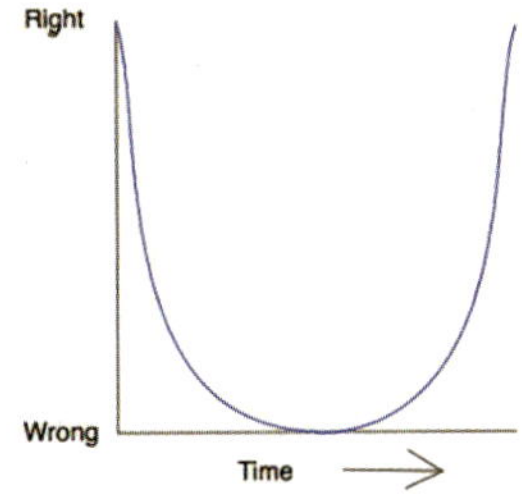

U-shaped Learning Curve

Errors are a natural part of learning. They usually show that learners are learning and that their internal mental processes are working on and experimenting with language. We go through stages of learning new language and each new piece of language we learn helps us learn other pieces of language that we already know more fully—like pieces of a jigsaw puzzle which only make full sense when they are all in place.

Developmental errors and errors of interference can disappear by themselves, without correction, as the learner learns more language. In fact, correction may only help learners if they are **primed*** for it, i.e., they are at the right stage in their individual learning process. But experts believe that learners can be helped to develop their interlanguage. There are three main ways of doing this. First, learners need exposure to lots of interesting language at the right level; second, they need to use language with other people; and finally, they need to focus their attention on the forms of language.

Sometimes errors do not disappear, but get fossilized. Fossilized errors are errors which a learner does not stop making and which last for a long time, even for ever, in his foreign language use. They often happen when learners, particularly adults, are able to communicate as much as they need to in the foreign language and so have no communicative reason to improve their language. These fossilized errors may be the result of lack of exposure to the L2 (second language) and/or of a learner's lack of motivation to improve their level of proficiency.

1 Key Vocabulary

lexis ***n.*** all of the words in a language
pass off ***v.*** to come to a gradual end
primed ***adj.*** prepared for immediate action or use

2 Complete the sentence using the correct form of the words in the box.

experiment	expose	complete	communicate	improve

a. On successful __________ of the sole language learning course, students will gain the ability to analyse and criticise one's own work.
b. Student attitudes towards language learning has __________ considerably and they show every sign of enjoying the experience.
c. In humans, it has been argued that social interaction is critical for language learning, but few __________ data exist to test the hypothesis.
d. If you listen twice as much as you talk, you come across as a good __________.
e. In the 1970s, it was a common assumption that __________ to more than one language would confuse young children and could lead to delays in learning to read.

3 Famous Quotes about Language

Q Think like a wise man but communicate in the language of the people. — William Butler Yeats

Q If you talk to a man in a language he understands, that goes to his head. If you talk to him in his language, that goes to his heart. — Nelson Mandela

Q French is the language that turns dirt into romance. — Stephen King

Q The only language men ever speak perfectly is the one they learn in babyhood, when no one can teach them anything! — Maria Montessori

Q It's my belief we developed language because of our deep inner need to complain. — Lily Tomlin

4 Find synonyms for the following words and circle them in the puzzle.

influence, normal, disappear, obvious, internal, improve

E	R	Y	Y	A	V	V	V	J	N	K
X	D	L	F	J	Y	W	A	G	X	K
V	S	E	E	Q	P	B	N	E	J	M
L	G	V	F	N	U	M	I	O	H	E
T	T	I	I	F	H	U	S	W	C	I
E	L	D	D	N	E	A	H	J	U	K
K	G	E	T	T	S	C	N	G	W	N
C	D	N	W	V	K	I	T	C	X	R
H	U	T	A	H	N	R	D	M	E	P
H	D	D	P	Z	I	U	K	E	K	G
H	U	S	U	A	L	P	P	U	H	A

HUMOR

1. A missionary goes to Africa to visit a community, a very old, primitive tribal community. He gives a long sermon. For half an hour he tells a long anecdote, and then the interpreter stands up. He speaks only four words and everyone laughs uproariously. The missionary is puzzled. How is it possible that a story half an hour long can be translated in four words? What kind of amazing language is this? Puzzled, he says to the interpreter, "You have done a miracle. You have spoken only four words. I don't know what you said, but how can you translate my story, which was so long, into only four words?" The interpreter says, "Story too long, so I say, 'He says joke — laugh!'"

2. A professor attempting to inspire his students says to his class, "This week is your last chance to study for your final exam next Monday. Time is running out. The exam is now in the hands of the printer. Are there any questions?" One student inquires, "How many questions will there be?" Another student asks, "Will the exam require essay answers?" A third wants to know, "Who's the printer?"

Nonverbal communication

Nonverbal communication involves those nonverbal stimuli in a communication setting that are generated by both the source (speaker) and his or her use of the environment and that have potential message value for the source or receiver (listener). Basically it is sending and receiving messages in a variety of ways without the use of verbal codes (words). It is both intentional and unintentional. Most speakers/listeners are not conscious of this. It includes—but is not limited to: touch, glance, eye contact, volume, vocal nuance, proximity, gestures, facial expression, intonation, dress, posture, smell, word choice and syntax, and sounds (paralanguage). Broadly speaking, there are two basic categories of non-verbal language: nonverbal messages produced by the body and those produced by the broad setting (time, space, silence).

Why is non-verbal communication important?

Basically, it is one of the key aspects of communication and especially important in a **high-context culture***. It has multiple functions:

- Used to repeat the verbal message (e.g., point in a direction while stating directions).
- Often used to accent a verbal message (e.g., verbal tone indicates the actual meaning of the specific words).
- Often complement the verbal message but also may contradict (e.g., a nod reinforces a positive message (among Americans); a "wink" may contradict a stated positive message).
- Regulate interactions (non-verbal cues convey when the other person should speak or not speak).
- May substitute for the verbal message, especially should it be blocked by noise, interruption, etc—i.e., gestures (finger to lips to indicate need for silence), facial expressions (i.e., a nod instead of a yes).

Cultural Differences in Non-verbal Communication

1. General Appearance and Dress

All cultures are concerned for how they look and make judgements based on looks and dress. Americans, for instance, appear almost obsessed with dress and personal attractiveness. Consider differing cultural standards on what is attractive in dress and on what constitutes modesty.

2. Body Movement

We send information on attitude toward person (facing or leaning towards another), emotional statue (tapping fingers, jiggling coins), and desire to control the environment (moving towards or away from a person). More than 700,000 possible motions we can make—so impossible to categorize them all! But just need to be aware the body movement and position is a key ingredient in sending messages.

3. Posture

Consider the following actions and note cultural differences:

- Bowing (not done, criticized, or affected in US; shows rank in Japan)
- **Slouching*** (rude in most Northern European areas)
- Hands in pocket (disrespectful in Turkey)
- Sitting with legs crossed (offensive in Ghana, Turkey)
- Showing soles of feet (offensive in Thailand, Saudi Arabia)

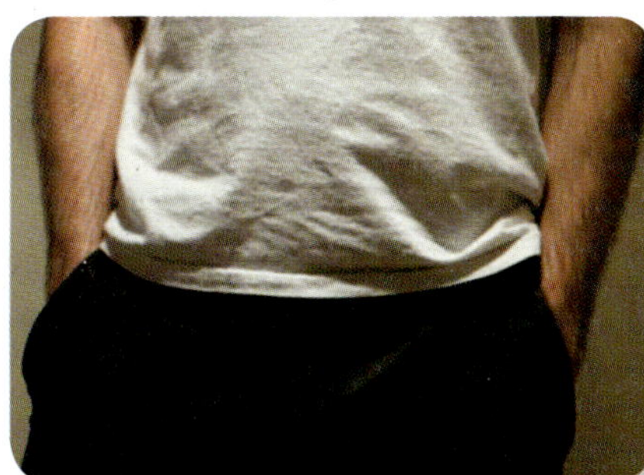

4. Gestures

It is impossible to catalogue them all. But you need to recognize that there is incredible possibility and variety and that an acceptable gesture in one's own culture may be offensive in another. In addition, amount of gesturing varies from culture to culture. Some cultures are animated; others restrained. Restrained cultures often feel animated cultures lack manners and overall restraint. Animated cultures often feel restrained cultures lack emotion or interest.

5. Facial Expressions

While some say that facial expressions are identical, meaning attached to them differs. Majority opinion is that these do have similar meanings world-wide with respect to smiling, crying, or showing anger, sorrow, or disgust. However, the intensity varies from culture to culture. Note the following:

- Many Asian cultures **suppress*** facial expression as much as possible.

- Many Mediterranean cultures exaggerate grief or sadness while most American men hide grief or sorrow.
- Some see animated expressions as a sign of a lack of control.
- Too much smiling is viewed as a sign of shallowness.

6. Eye Contact and Gaze

In USA, eye contact indicates degree of attention or interest, influences attitude change or persuasion, regulates interaction, communicates emotion, defines power and status, and has a central role in managing impressions of others.

- Western cultures see direct eye to eye contact as positive (advise children to look a person in the eyes). But within USA, African-Americans use more eye contact when talking and less when listening with reverse true for Anglo Americans. This is a possible cause for some sense of unease between races in US. A prolonged gaze is often seen as a sign of sexual interest.

- Arabic cultures make prolonged eye contact. They believe it shows interest and helps them understand truthfulness of the other person. A person who doesn't **reciprocate*** is seen as untrustworthy.
- Africa, Latin American, Caribbean—avoid eye contact to show respect.

7. Touch

Basic message of touch is to affect or control—protect, support, disapprove (i.e., hug, kiss, hit, kick). And each culture has a clear concept of what parts of the body one may not touch.

- USA: Handshake is common (even for strangers), hugs, kisses for those of opposite gender or of family (usually) on an increasingly more intimate basis. Note differences between African-Americans and Anglos in USA. Most African Americans touch on greeting but are annoyed if touched on the head (good boy, good girl overtones).

- Islamic and Hindu: They typically don't touch with the left hand. To do so is a social insult. Left hand is for toilet functions. Islamic cultures generally don't approve of any touching between genders (even handshakes). But consider such touching (including hand holding, hugs) between same-sex to be appropriate.
- Many Asians don't touch the head. Head houses the soul and a touch puts it in jeopardy.

8. Smell

- USA: Fear of offensive natural smells (billion dollar industry to mask objectionable odors with what is perceived to be pleasant)
- Many other cultures (Arabic) consider natural body odors as normal.
- Asian cultures (Filipino, Malay, Indonesian, Thai, Indian) stress frequent bathing—and often criticize USA of not bathing often enough!

9. Paralanguage

- Vocal characterizers (laugh, cry, yell, moan, whine, belch, yawn). These send different messages in different cultures (Japan—giggling indicates embarrassment; India—belch indicates satisfaction).
- vocal qualifiers (volume, pitch, rhythm, tempo, and tone). Loudness indicates strength in Arabic cultures and softness indicates weakness.
- vocal segregates (un-huh, shh, uh, ooh, mmmh, humm, eh, mah, lah). Segregates indicate formality, acceptance, **assent***, or uncertainty.

1 Key Vocabulary

high context culture *n.* High context culture and the contrasting low context culture are terms presented by the anthropologist Edward T. Hall. It refers to a culture's tendency to use high context messages over low context messages in routine communication. In a high context culture, many things are left unsaid, letting the culture explain. Words and word choice become very important in higher context communication, since a few words can communicate a complex message very effectively to an in-group (but less effectively outside that group), while in a lower context culture, the communicator needs to be much more explicit and the value of a single word is less important. (Source: Adapted from the website http://en.wikipedia.org/wiki/High_context_culture)

slouching ***n.*** sitting or standing with an awkward, bent posture
suppress ***v.*** to prohibit; to stop the activities of
reciprocate ***v.*** to interchange; to give in response
assent ***n.*** agreement; consent

2 For each word in Group A, find the corresponding synonym in Group B and antonym in Group C.

Group A	Synonym	Antonym
a. generate		
b. contradict		
c. truthfulness		
d. mask(v.)		
e. jeopardy		
f. difference		

Group B. Synonym	Group C. Antonym
sincerity	unveil
disguise	falseness
deviate	annihilate
initiate	security
contrast	resemblance
peril	endorse

3 Grammar Focus

> Nonverbal communication may substitute for the verbal message, especially ***should it be blocked by noise or interruption***.

Should occurs in conditional clauses with *if* in formal contexts, expressing tentative possibilities. *Should* also occurs with subject-verb inversion as an alternative to *if* in more formal contexts to refer to hypothetical situations.

a. *If* you *should* happen to have a forecast of heavy rain to come, there is no where to hide around there.

b. *If* you *should* need anything further, please don't hesitate to ask.
c. I can send you more pictures *should* you need them.
d. What are the issues you want me to address *should* you hire me?

4 **Rude hand gestures around the world** (Source: Adapted from the website www.k9keystrokes.hubpages.com)

Meaning: Are you an idiot?
Where: Brazil

Meaning: Piss off!
Where: Belgium, France

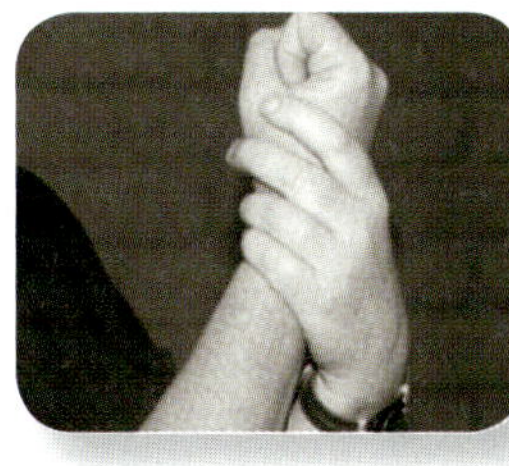

Meaning: Stick it up!
Where: Lebanon, Syria

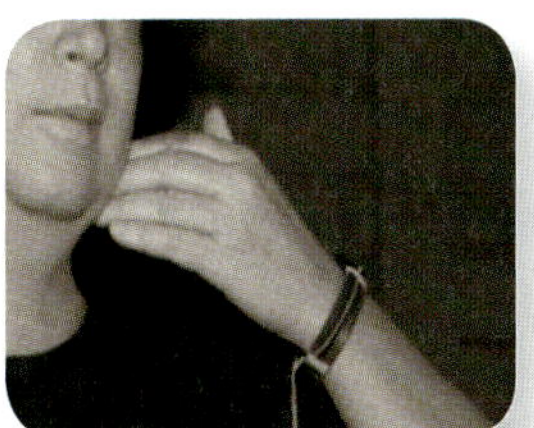

Meaning: I'm getting bored.
Where: France

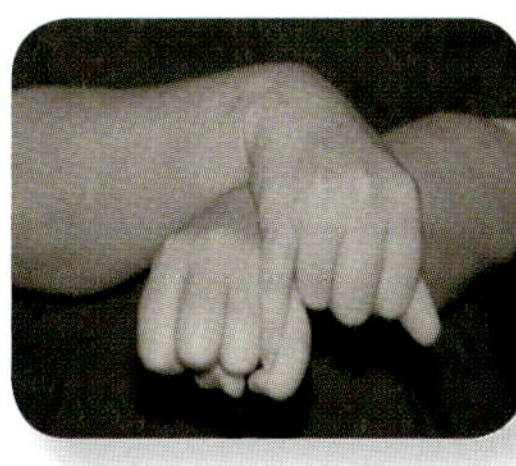

Meaning: I can't trust you.
Where: Southern Italy

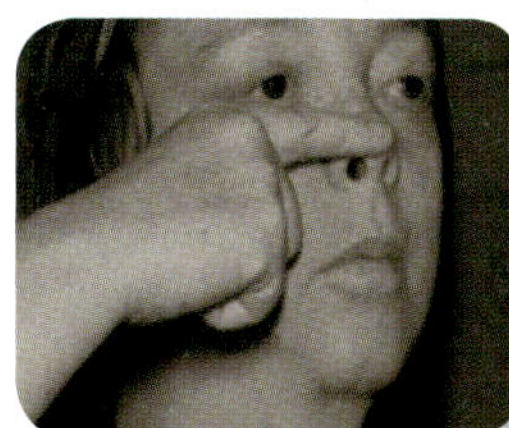

Meaning: You're ugly.
Where: Japan

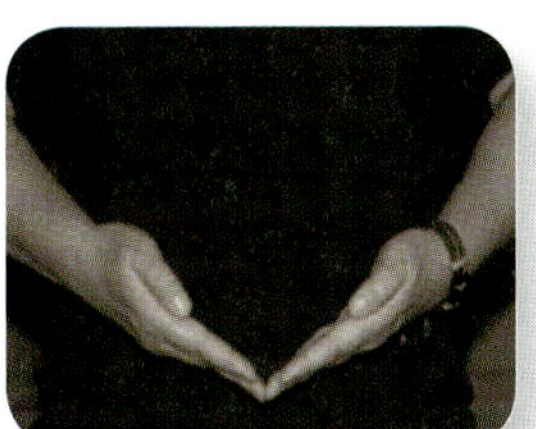

Meaning: I ignore you.
Where: Greece

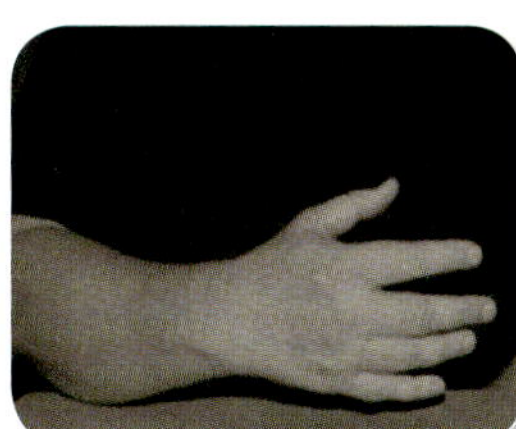

Meaning: dirty thief
Where: South America

Meaning: Shut your mouth!
Where: France, USA

Jokes about learning

1. The teacher of the earth science class was lecturing on map reading. After explaining about latitude, longitude, degrees and minutes the teacher asked, "Suppose I asked you to meet me for lunch at 23 degrees, 4 minutes north latitude and 45 degrees, 15 minutes east longitude ...?" After a confused silence, a voice volunteered, "I guess you'd be eating alone."

2. Two factory workers talking:
Woman: "I can make the boss give me the day off."
Man: "And how would you do that?"
Woman: "Just wait and see."
She then hangs upside-down from the ceiling.
Boss comes in: "What are you doing?"
Woman: "I'm a light bulb."
Boss: "You've been working so much that you've got **cracked***. I think you need to take the day off."
The man starts to follow her and the boss says: "Where are you going?"
The man says: "I'm going home, too. I can't work in the dark."

3. A professor was traveling by boat. On his way he asked the sailor:
"Do you know Biology, Ecology, Zoology, Geography, Physiology?"
The sailor said no to all his questions.

Professor: "What the hell do you know on earth? You will die of illiteracy."
After a while the boat started sinking. The sailor asked the professor, "Do you know swiminology & escapology from sharkology?"
The professor said no.
Sailor: "Well, sharkology & crocodilogy will eat your assology, headology & you will dieology because of your mouthology."

4. A police officer stopped a car which

was **weaving*** alarmingly and asked the driver what he was doing. "I am learning to drive," was the reply. "What? without an instructor?" exclaimed the officer. "Oh yes," answered the driver. "It's a correspondence course."

5. A mathematician organizes a raffle in which the prize is an infinite amount of money paid over an infinite amount of time. Of course, with the promise of such a prize, his tickets sell like hot cake. When the winning ticket is drawn, and the **jubilant*** winner comes to claim his prize, the mathematician explains the mode of payment: "1 dollar now, 1/2 dollar next week, 1/3 dollar the week after that ..."

6. Two college seniors had a week of exams coming up. They decided to party instead. Their biggest exam was on Wednesday and they showed up telling the professor that their car had broken down the night before due to a very flat tire and they needed a bit more time to study. The professor told them that they could have another day to study. That evening, both of the boys crammed all night until they were sure that they knew just about everything. Arriving to class the next morning, each boy was told to go to two separate classrooms to take the exam. Each boy just shrugged and went to two different parts of the building. As each sat down, they read the first question. "For 5 points, explain the contents of an atom." At this point, they both thought that this was going to be **rudimentary***, and answered the question with ease. Then, the test continued. "For 95 points, tell me which tire it was."

7. Q: How is a dog and a marine biologist alike?
   A: One wags a tail and the other tags a whale.

1 Key Vocabulary

cracked ***adj.*** being crazy(slang)
weave ***v.*** to make a way by winding in and out or from side to side
jubilant ***adj.*** full of delight
rudimentary ***adj.*** relating to basic facts or principles

2 Answer the following questions related to the above jokes.

a. # 2: If you are the boss, would you give a day off to the man who followed the woman? Why or why not?

____

____

b. # 4: What other excuse would the drive give to the police officer when he was caught for reckless driving?

____

____

c. # 5: How would the winner react to the mathematician's explanation about the mode of payment?

____

____

d. # 6: Provided that you're one of the two students, what would you write when you get the question, "Which tire was it?"

____

____

Supplement

ANSWER KEY

Vocabulary Index

Credits

ANSWER KEY

P. 7 Exercise 2

a. unripe
b. scratched
c. tempting
d. grasp
e. dent
f. crunched

P. 10 Exercise 2

a. attractive
b. attributable
c. popularity
d. traditional
e. specializes
f. specifically
g. preferable
h. literally

P. 12 Cross-Word Puzzle

Across
1. spread
6. specialty
7. attraction
9. roll
10. humble
12. premise

Down
1. slope
2. authentic
3. venture
4. poisonous
5. diameter
8. topping
11. evoke

P. 15 Exercise 2

1. his tins = canned soups or tuna
2. health supplements = protein shake, calcium
3. his modest rooms ... how crying out for change = untidy, messed up
4. 12 cans of lager = beer, malt liquor
5. He must need basics = toothbrush, shampoo

P. 17 Exercise 2

a. false; A fattier fish does not need moist heat.
b. false; A firm-fleshed fish is a good choice for the grill because it holds together well.
c. false; 24 minutes is recommended (cf. 1 inch of thickness requires 12 minutes.).
d. true

P. 18 Cross-Word Puzzle

Across
3. muffin
4. cereal
6. hamburger
9. sushi
10. potato
11. taco

Down
1. pizza
2. rice
4. cheese
5. egg

7. banana
8. milk

P. 22 Exercise 2
a. increasingly
b. specifically
c. effectively
d. inadequately
e. chronically
f. separately

P. 27 Exercise 3
1. weigh
2. quantities
3. self-induced
4. compensate
5. slightly
6. desperately

P. 31 Exercise 2
a. boss
b. borrow
c. push
d. lie
e. easy
f. stand

P. 31 Exercise 3
a. architects
b. harbourmasters
c. flight attendants
d. security guards
e. conductors
f. foresters

P. 34 Exercise 4
1. traits
2. type
3. hates
4. dumb
5. lips
6. reputation
7. notice

P. 37 Exercise 2
a. young
b. old
c. young
d. old
e. young

P. 38 Exercise 4
1. f
2. g
3. e
4. b
5. h
6. c
7. d
8. a

P. 41 Exercise 2
a. avoid
b. cover
c. alter
d. lasting
e. dismissed

P. 41 Exercise 3
a. false
b. true
c. false

P. 49 Exercise 2
a. experimental
b. contingent
c. artifact
d. divine

e. subsume
f. catalyst
g. reinforcement
h. humanistic

P. 49 Exercise 3
cognitivism

P. 51 Cross-Word Puzzle
Across
1. upset
3. happy
4. anxious
8. delighted
10. furious
11. cheerful

Down
2. surprised
4. angry
5. scary
6. pleased
7. nervous
8. depressed
9. proud

P. 56 Exercise 2
a. tactics
b. accommodate
c. inventory
d. availability
e. offset
f. revoked
g. deems

P. 58 Exercise 5
a. substitute = alternative ↔ irreplaceable
b. claim = postulate ↔ retract
c. endemic = rife ↔ sporadic
d. dilute = thin ↔ fortify
e. substantial = considerable ↔ meager
f. worry = vex ↔ soothe
g. vary = diversify ↔ constrict

P. 67 Exercise 3
a. furious > crazy
b. correct
c. he understood > he never understood
d. correct

P. 71 Exercise 2
a. sprinkler
b. thermometer
c. washing machine
d. credit card
e. eraser
f. hair dryer
g. microscope
h. TV remote control

P. 76 Exercise 2
a. car
b. gum
c. airline
d. coffee
e. fast food
f. cereal
g. soap
h. toothpaste
i. diaper

P. 79 Exercise 2
a. third place
b. innovation
c. perfect cup of coffee
d. brand marketing

P. 79 Exercise 3

a. definite = explicit ↔ vague
b. satisfying = adequate ↔ insufficient
c. uniqueness = singularity ↔ unoriginality
d. encourage = boost ↔ depress
e. grow = expand ↔ diminish
f. capability = potential ↔ incompetence

P. 85 Exercise 2

a. alley
b. trend
c. fragile
d. banquet
e. cutback
f. favor

P. 85 Exercise 3

a. true
b. spring > summer
c. no > some
d. true
e. true

P. 91 Exercise 3

a. true
b. false
c. true
d. false
e. false
f. false
g. true

P. 99 Exercise 2

a. peril = hazard ↔ security
b. socialize = mingle ↔ isolate
c. ally = colleague ↔ opponent
d. obscure = ambiguous ↔ apparent
e. trustworthy = dependable ↔ disloyal
f. enrage = provoke ↔ soothe
g. triumph = accomplishment ↔ disaster

P. 100 Exercise 3

A 1 → B 2
A 2 → B 5
A 3 → B 1
A 4 → B 3
A 5 → B 4

P. 101 Exercise 4

a. recommended
b. don't tell the colleague > tell the colleague
c. as virtues in themselves, not as tools to career advancement > not just as virtues in themselves, but as tools to career advancement
d. recommended

P. 108 Exercise 2

a. style consultants
b. a tool in her diplomatic arsenal (referring to fashion)
c. some unknown people who searched the palace after she had been kicked out of the palace
d. avoiding that ... to the complexion
e. (political) subtext

P. 109 Exercise 3

a. aesthetic
b. deserve
c. benchmark
d. twist
e. eggplant
f. set apart
g. silhouette

P. 114 Exercise 2

a. impression
b. idleness

c. rarely
d. owner
e. harden
f. invention
g. environment
h. gradually

P. 115 Exercise 3
a. opinion
b. fact
c. opinion
d. opinion

P. 120 Cross-Word Puzzle
Across
1. fragile
4. grip
5. launch
6. wrench
8. abate
10. expel

Down
1. foil
2. evocative
3. screw
4. gaiety
7. hiss
9. remnant

P. 124 Exercise 2
a. crutches
b. tailored
c. resolve
d. vaguely
e. tote
f. dampened

P. 124 Exercise 3
a. Wall Street turning into one big fire sale
b. Hermès sample sale
c. Not buying anything
d. another Hermès scarf
e. every other rationale for buying something

P. 126 Exercise 6
1. significant = important
2. bargain = agreement
3. brag = boast
4. comply = follow
5. absurd = ridiculous
6. bolster = support

P. 130 Exercise 2
a. personalities
b. dominate
c. primitive
d. game

P. 134 Exercise 2
a. deter
b. fine
c. consequence
d. internal
e. disapproval
f. stare

P. 137 Exercise 2
1. b
2. a
3. b
4. c

P. 141 Exercise 2
a. roar
b. recede

c. salute
d. rub
e. barely

P. 147 Exercise 3
a. mutter
b. slam
c. rush
d. frustration
e. rage
f. menacing
g. predator

P. 153 Exercise 2
a. maintainable
b. deteriorative
c. stimulative
d. communicative
e. considerate
f. encouraging
g. treatable
h. engaging

P. 154 Exercise 3
a. true
b. early stage > later stages
c. Even with Alzheimer's disease, people are able to verbally express their likes and dislikes. > With Alzheimer's disease, people may not be able to verbally communicate their likes and dislikes.
d. true
e. visiting with a dog > petting a cat

P. 157 Cross-Word Puzzle
Across
2. distant
4. lavish
8. daunting
10. repay
11. revival

Down
1. fascinate
3. column
5. heyday
6. refund
7. original
9. report

P. 161 Exercise 2
a. attractive
b. exhibition
c. inequality
d. international
e. homelessness
f. prehistoric
g. encourage
h. randomly

P. 166 Exercise 2
a. draw
b. precaution
c. tumbled
d. drag
e. sequence
f. considered
g. edge

P. 172 Exercise 2
a. completion
b. improved
c. experimental
d. communicator
e. exposure

P. 172 Exercise 4

1. influence = effect
2. normal = usual
3. disappear = vanish
4. obvious = evident
5. internal = inside
6. improve = enhance

P. 178 Exercise 2

a. generate = initiate ↔ annihilate
b. contradict = deviate ↔ endorse
c. truthfulness = sincerity ↔ falseness
d. mask = disguise ↔ unveil
e. jeopardy = peril ↔ security
f. difference = contrast ↔ resemblance

Vocabulary Index

erode
must
offbeat
pass off
phony
pinch one's pennies
pitch
ramp up
sample
seamstress
tacky
undercover
usher
venue
viral
whittle
word-of-mouth

Chapter 6
affinity
antic
Barneys
burn a few/one's bridges
canny
catapult
chirp
conscientious
couture
credentials
disarmament
discreet
doormat
eccentric
elocution
emulate
fixate
glad-handing
go
heist
hemline
hideous
homicide
HR
hunker
impervious
insouciance
intriguing
Jackie O
jazz up
jockey
keep one's nose to the grindstone
marginalized
meme
moon
needling
nemesis
nudge
nugget
on board
pathological
peripheral
provenance
rarefy
rector
rootin'-tootin'
rowdy
sewage
skeleton
subtext
toot one's horn
transparency
Tumblr
unleash
verge
vibe

Chapter 7
abate
alienated
bolster
champagne wrench
circumscribe
cove
demur
Escalades
fire sale
gaiety
hop out
hover
knockoff
malaise
perennial
prematurely
reckon
resolve
shed
showcase
sporadic
temporal
tote
ubiquitous
umbilical

Chapter 8
beat-up
bleary
cloud
cramped
date
despairingly
disapproval
enunciate
imprisonment
imprudent
lapel

Chapter 9

Chapter 10

Credits

p. 6	Adapted from *When I was Puerto Rican* by E. Santiago. 1996. Da Capo Press. p. 3-4. Reprinted with permission.
p. 8-10	Adapted from the website http://en.wikipedia.org/wiki/History_of_pizza.
p. 13-14	Adapted from *The Devil's Larder* by J. Crace. 2001. Farrar, Straus and Giroux. p. 21. Reprinted with permission.
p. 16	Adapted from the website http://www.greateasternsfd.com/page/menu_5/11369.html.
p. 19-21	Adapted from the website http://www.blackjackair.com/indoor-air-quality/
p. 22-23	Adapted from the website http://en.wikipedia.org/wiki/Category:Syndromes.
p. 24-25	Adapted from the website http://kidshealth.org/teen/your_mind/mental_ health/eat_disorder.html.
p. 27	From www.nimh.nih.gov/health/publications/eating-disorders/complete-index.html.
p. 30	Adapted from the website http://www.shorewood.k12.wi.us/page.cfm?p=3586.
p. 31	Adapted from the website http://en.wikipedia.org.
p. 32	Adapted from the website http://www.iile.ru/library/meth/m559.rtf.
p. 34	Adapted from the website http://www.careerbuilder.com/Article/CB-1167-The-Workplace-Your-Negative-Attitude-Can-Hurt-Your-Career.
p. 36	Adapted from *The Writings of Oliver Wendell Holmes* by O. Holmes. 1891. Riverside Press. p. 377.
p. 38	Adapted from the website http://thejokes.co.uk/jokes-about-doctors-6.php.
p. 40	Adapted from *Is your partner lying to you?* by McClatchy Newspapers. 2009. Jan. 12. Reprinted with permission.
p. 43-48	Adapted from the website http://en.wikipedia.org/wiki/Psychology.
p. 52-56	Adapted from the website http://www.slideshare.net/leader443/consumer-psychology-and-pricing.
p. 62	Adapted from the website http://www.strangemag.com/highstrangenesstimetrav.html.
p. 65-66	Adapted from *Who got Eisenstein's office?* by E. Regis. 2000. Addison-Wesley. p. 19-20. Reprinted with permission.
p. 69	Adapted from "Who made Velcro?" by P. Kennedy. 2012. *The New York Times*. November 9. Reprinted with permission.
p. 74-75	Adapted from the website https://www.thirstt.com/tbooks/Typesof-Guerrilla-Marketing/53e706482695dc360935a004.
p. 77-78	Adapted from the website http://www.voteforus.com/starbucksmarketing strategy.html.
p. 80	Adapted from the website http://en.mimi.hu/marketingweb/index_marketingweb.html.
p. 81-84	Adapted from the website http://www.wibw.com/home/headlines/98314369.html.
p. 88-90	Adapted from "Academic turns city into a social experiment" by M, Caballero. 2004. *Harvard University Gazette*. March 11. Reprinted with permission.
p. 92	From http://thejokes.co.uk/jokes-about-politicians-3.php.
p. 93-98	Adapted from the website http://www.wetfeet.com/advice-tools/on-the-job/how-to-deal-with-office-politics.

p. 100 From http://www.bitoffun.com/jokes_office.htm.

p. 102-106 Adapted from "10 Powerful Fashion Statements Made by Women in Politics" by M. Lepore. 2012. *The Grindstone*. September 5. Reprinted with permission.

p. 112-113 Adapted from "Vacations let us loosen time's grip" by E. Goodman. 1987. *The Courier*. August, 26.

p. 117-118 Adapted from "Champagne corks should never take off, for safety or taste" by *The Wilmington Morning Star*. 1982. Dec. 31. Reprinted with permission.

p. 121-123 Adapted from "A Sample Sale at Hermès Defies the Wall Street Malaise" by S. Dominus. 2008. *The New York Times*. September 25. Reprinted with permission.

p. 128-129 Adapted from *Reading at the University* by L. Hillman. 1990. Heinle & Heinle. p. 209-210. Reprinted with permission.

p. 131 From http://www.ahajokes.com.

p. 132-133 Adapted from the website http://engtopic.ru/english-language/controllingcrime-what-stops-us-from-committing-crimes.

p. 136 Adapted from the website http://www.nexuslearning.net/books/holt_elementsoflit3/Collection%207/Darkness%20at%20Noon.htm.

p. 137 Adapted from the website http://baloch3995.blogspot.kr/2013/06/dog.html.

p. 139-140 Adapted from "The Wallet" by A. McCuaig. 2003. *Beloit Fiction Journal(16)*. p. 234.

p. 142 From http://thejokes.co.uk/jokes-about-car-drivers.php.

p. 144-146 Adapted from "Victims Versus Oppressors" by C. DeLeon. 1985. *The Philadelphia Inquirer*. February 5. Reprinted with permission.

p. 147 Adapted from the website http://zumaworld.blogspot.kr/2011/07/threats-mario-puzo.html.

p. 150-152 Adapted from http://www.webmd.com/alzheimers/alzheimerstherapies-music-art-more. Reprinted with permission.

p. 155 Adapted from the website http://svetlanareznikova79.narod.ru.

p. 156 Adapted from the website http://en.wikipedia.org/wiki/Gossip.

p. 158-160 Adapted from the website http://learnenglishteens.britishcouncil.org/study-break/easy-reading/graffitiand-street-art-level-3.

p. 164-165 Adapted from "School of hard knocks Toronto stunt school teaches safe crash courses" by P, Cheney. 1989. *The Toronto Star*, January 14. Reprinted with permission.

p. 166-167 Adapted from the website www.wikipedia.org.

p. 170-171 Adapted from the website http://www.slideshare.net/JennyYon/the-tkt-teaching.

p. 173 Adapted from the websites http://www.andreabecca.it and http://thejokes.co.uk/jokes-about-education-3.php.

p. 174-177 Adapted from the website http://www.andrews.edu/~tidwell/bsad560/Non Verbal.html.

p. 180-181 Adapted from the websites http://academictips.org/funny-jokes/and http://manish-jay.blogspot.kr/2011/07/jokes-on-education.html.

Every effort has been made to trace the owners of copyright materials in this book. However, if any has been overlooked inadvertently, I will be pleased to make the necessary arrangements.

Kyung Suk Kim

Professor, Dept. of English Language and Literature,
Kyonggi University
BA in English Education, Korea University
MA in TESOL, University of Illinois at Urbana-Champaign
PhD in Educational Linguistics, University of Pennsylvania

FOCUSED READING

SHINASA Publishing Co.
4, Tongil-ro 59-gil Eunpyeong-gu Seoul, Republic of Korea
Tel : 02)382-6411
Fax : 02)382-6401
E - MAIL: shinasa@daum.net
Homepage : www.shinasa.co.kr

First published April, 2015

ISBN 978-89-8396-900-2(93740)

Price : ₩*15,000*